Understanding
Border Collies

Understanding
Border Collies

Barbara Sykes

The Crowood Press

First published in 1999 by
The Crowood Press Ltd
Ramsbury, Marlborough
Wiltshire SN8 2HR
enquiries@crowood.com
www.crowood.com

This impression 2021

British Library Cataloguing-in-Publication Data
A catalogue record for this book is available from the British Library

ISBN 978 1 86126 280 6

Dedication
This book is dedicated to all the great Sheepdogs of the past, for they are the ancestors of the present day Border Collies, who in turn are the foundation dogs of the future. We owe it to them to make sure their intelligence, loyalty and stamina lives on for future generations to enjoy.

Acknowledgements
I would like to thank Malcolm and Maureen for their photographic skills and their patience. Without their help the cover and many of the photographs in this book would not have been possible. I would also like to thank Caroline for her time in reproducing my 'mental' pictures so well in her graphics, and Pat Borrows whose poetry can bring a collie to life. I am most grateful to Gilbertson and Page who provided invaluable nutritional support. And last but by no means least I must thank my son and daughter, Gary and Vicki, whose support over the years has given me the courage to stand up for my beliefs.

Photographs supplied by Malcolm and Maureen Merone, Trevor Robinson, Betty Duggan, and the author.

Graphics – Caroline Simpson

Typeset by The Florence Group, Stoodleigh, Devon
Printed and bound in India by Replika Press Pvt. Ltd.

Contents

The Voices in the Blood

He's only your pet Collie, romping on a sunlit lawn,
Or sleeping on the rug before the fire.
Though his role in life is just to be friend beyond compare,
He's a servant more than worthy of his hire.
For if his fate should call him to a dozen different tasks,
He could do each one incomparably well;
Adapting to each changed demand, intelligent and keen,
In all things he is destined to excel.

You might see him in Obedience and watch him winning Crufts,
Or in Working Trials, achieving T.D.ex,
Or racing through Agility, (and he could be a bitch,
For competence does not depend on sex!)
You could mark his patient searching in a devastated town,
Through the ruins that an earthquake leaves behind.
Or proud in his white harness, see him walk the city streets,
A rare, but special Guide Dog for the Blind.

He may never even glimpse the sheep that he was bred to herd,
(As Mountain Rescue Dog he would ignore them!)
But all true collies listen to the voices in their blood
Of ancestors who proudly went before them.
He is able to diversify because of what he is,
From his long history derives his worth.
Guide, searcher, champion, yes! But first of all
The best and wisest herding dog on earth.

So understand him if one day an ancient memory stirs,
And he casts out round a most indignant cat!
And does his level best to bring her in to you, because
His long dead forebears told him to do that.
There are those who would attempt to breed his herding instinct out,
Dismissing it as something they don't need.
If they don't want the working genes that make him what he is
They'd do well to find themselves another breed.

Though he's only your pet Collie, fast asleep before the fire,
Or playing with the children on the lawn;
Still Man has no right to silence those voices in his blood,
That remind him of the reason he was born.

Pat Borrows

Introduction

The Border Collie is a versatile and popular breed, and is capable of adapting to many different lifestyles. This book is not about training for one of the many disciplines, nor is it intended to teach one person's method of training – just as different dogs need handling in different ways, so handlers need to develop their own style. This individual style rests primarily on the person involved, but must also include the ability to adapt to their dog's requirements. The Border Collie is a herding dog – a sheepdog – and this must always be taken into account when training. If the intention of a trainer is to ignore or squash these instincts, he is not only depriving the collie of its natural instincts but is subduing it, which will make it submissive rather than biddable.

This book gives an insight into the mind of the Border Collie and how it thinks; the pack instincts are explained in detail and in some cases have been simplified for ease of understanding. Training is not complicated and it is fun if you are working with your dog rather than against it. Whether you are bringing up a puppy or training an older dog, the 'common sense' training methods in this book apply to both – they provide a foundation for more advanced training, enabling the reader to continue into any of the disciplines with a sensible, well-educated dog.

You may be a keen competitor or an energetic walker, you may be a sheepdog handler or a first-time dog owner, you may need your dog to work or to be solely a companion. Whatever your intentions, if you love this breed of dog you will be fascinated as you find out not only more about them, but also how to understand them when you take a look inside their minds through the pages of this book.

CHAPTER 1

What is a Collie?

While collies are different to most other breeds of dog, they are still derived from pack origins. We may have some 'man-made' breeds which are the result of various crossing or mixing, but the true breeds all originate from a similar source. In all breeds, the training methods should still adhere to what the dog understands and not what we humans think it should understand! The Border Collie is derived from the wolf and has strong pack instincts; our ancestors have taken great care when breeding with their collies to keep these instincts strong to provide a perfect working, shepherding partner. Because of these instincts we have a dual responsibility, one to those people who have, and still do, breed a beautiful, intelligent and strong work dog, to keep the breed true to its origins; and secondly to the dog itself, to understand it and help it to understand us!

Different lifestyles of the Border Collie

We only have to look at the many different lifestyles of the modern-day Border Collie to appreciate how very versatile the breed is. Puppies born of the same litter may lead lives that are totally different, going from the extremes of the hard-working farm dog to the family pet. Let us take a look at a few of these lifestyles and the way a day may start for some collies.

As the dawn mist moves gently across the fellside the shepherd and his two collies leave the warmth of the farm kitchen to tend their flock. The collies bound energetically around their master's feet. After a hard early morning's shepherding, in the afternoon they may be displaying their skills competitively at a local sheepdog trial.

Many miles away, on lower land, the dogs' cousin will use his herding powers for a different kind of shepherding. His skill will be employed to gather a herd of cattle into the farmyard and later in the day he will be accompanying his master in the cattle wagon on the journey to the local market. While these collies are using their natural instincts in everyday life, many more of their 'family' will be awakening to completely different lifestyles. Some may already be up, eager with anticipation as their owners pack the car with all the necessary equipment for a show. They will be displaying the collie's great versatility in agility, obedience, or any other of the popular dog sports. While these dogs are preparing for their sport, still more 'relations' will be out working or training for their employment in some of the many services where a dog's skills are required. Whilst their intelligence and adaptability is used to help mankind in search and rescue and

A Border Collie using the 'power of its eye' while working sheep. Note the front leg raised as it creeps quietly forwards.

as 'sniffer' dogs, their gentleness and sensitivity brings joy to many, in both hospitals and homes for the elderly, where employed as a registered 'Pat Dog': therapeutic stroking pleases both dog and patient. Many more collies, all distant relations to our 'workers on the hill', will still be in bed; their day will not entail being on anyone's 'payroll', and as companion collies (pets) they will spend an easy day in the house and garden, taking exercise with the family.

We have all seen members of the collie family employed in at least one of the above. Some readers may have a trophy to display, some may be sat on a chewed piece of furniture, and some may be wondering if a collie is the breed they should choose after all. A Border Collie is an extremely versatile breed of dog. He is faithful enough to be a loyal friend, honest enough to be a hard worker, and intelligent enough to be an asset in rescue and other services. He is also humorous and cheeky and will ensure you never have a dull moment!

Is it really possible to understand Border Collies? I believe so, but almost like a marriage a little mystery is not a bad thing, or so I was told! I don't think it would be in our best interests to know everything; even if it were possible, this breed is intelligent enough to have its own opinions and I think in some cases we may be better off not knowing what they are thinking! What we need to understand is how they work things out and why; for example, what they may happen to think about your choice of friend or your neighbour is not impor- tant, but why they have that opinion and how to deal with it is.

Information on the Border Collie as a breed is readily available from many sources, but it is important to remember that this is a sheepdog and as such has instincts which need understanding. If these instincts are not translated by the handler in the manner the dog intends, then mismanagement may occur; on the other hand, if the translation is correct the handler needs to control them in a manner the dog understands. To do this, we need to go back to our ancestral collies and use the time and experience of the past to help us to understand the present-day collies. But first, how much do we know about the dog itself?

Knowing is part way to understanding. If we pay little or no attention to the background of the breed we only have the present for information, and can we really rely on facts that may be based on human assumption rather than on the actual history of the breed? If we take time to find out about the dog's instincts, how it communicates and why it responds to certain situations and commands we are beginning to meet our dog 'halfway', the first steps to a partnership. There are so many questions and each one has a multitude of answers but, if we find out more, the correct answers are not too hard to find.

We know the Border Collie is an intelligent breed of dog with strong working instincts. He is very quick to learn – often too quick, leaving his unsuspecting handler in a whirl! From this knowledge we can be prepared for the dog to learn bad habits quickly and probably without the handler realizing until it is too late. The breed is known for the power of its eye, which we will discuss in a later chapter, but this knowledge should advise us to respect the dog's 'eye' and not have a confrontation. Herding is a natural instinct, so if the young dog is taken to where sheep, ducks or other livestock are roaming before adequate training has been given expect nature to take its course! It is also a breed full of stamina and great endurance, so it would be wise not to be misguided into walking miles everyday or an athletic collie will be produced which may be hard to keep up with. Most information on collies leads prospective owners to believe they must be prepared to walk miles to keep their dog exercised, but although a collie needs exercise, it does not need to be excessive – exercise of the mind is just as important. We know the breed is derived from pack origins and a pack dog does not set out to take long energetic walks everyday. They roam, graze (yes, graze) and idle. A pack dog also understands its own nutritional requirements and domestic collies are often fed on a diet which is far too energy-giving, resulting in a hyperactive dog and a distressed owner. A pack dog has one of two positions in the pack, that of pack leader or pack member, and we should know automatically that we need to be pack leader and the leader of any pack is always in front. So now we understand that we need to keep our dog behind us to establish our position.

Just look at how many questions we have answered and we have hardly begun! Some of those answers will probably have taken you a little by surprise. Some of the 'typical' collie facts have been explained in a different manner and we will handle them in a different way.

The reasons for wanting a collie are many and varied. They are intelligent, nice to look at and are faithful, but it is important to know what kind of intelligence you will be dealing with and how the collie's mind works. To learn how to do this, for a moment we must disregard the politics of registration, stud books or work versus pet and look at the collie himself, his instincts and how strongly they affect his behaviour.

Derived from pack origins, the collie's natural instincts are akin to that of the wolf, a predator. All stalking and herding instincts would culminate in the killing

The modern day Border Collie still carries a strong resemblance to its predatorial ancestors and has the ability to concentrate for long periods of time.

brain. Unable to run a hillside and gather sheep themselves, it became obvious to our ancestors that they needed a dog who had the stamina to run a mountain, the speed to outrun wayward sheep, and the courage to turn truculent ewes. In addition, they needed loyalty to work side by side with man, enduring long hours often in severe weather conditions, and the intelligence to understand a situation and act accordingly when alone with sheep miles from home. It mattered not what this dog looked like – colour, size (although too large a dog was not favourable), ears, coat length and texture, all were unimportant. The quality of the brain and nimbleness of body, coupled

The intelligence, loyalty, gentleness and stamina of Border Collies gives them natural beauty.

of the prey to appease the appetite. Through the years, man has channelled these instincts to form an intelligent, loyal shepherding assistant. From this information we can draw a picture of the collie throughout his formative years. Without going into the technical side of breeding and explained simply, our ancestors needed assistance in shepherding their stock and a cur without herding instinct was as useless as a predator that killed. Sheep needed then, as now, firm, gentle handling at close quarters and speed and stamina at a distance; above all, the shepherds needed a dog with

with loyalty, gentleness and stamina, became the criteria. Hence we have the working sheepdog now known as the Border Collie.

Having begun to understand why and how he was bred, let us now look at the Border Collie's way of life for the past century, and make the picture of him a little clearer. To do this, we must go back to before the days of cars, cattlewagons, portable races and other similar appliances that the modern-day shepherd has at his service. Our ancestral One Man with his Dogs would be equipped with a good pair of footwear and a crook; his day would begin at dawn and finish at dusk. Both man and dogs would be on their feet for most of their shepherding hours, walking round the flocks, gathering, lambing. Their working hours spent as a team, they would become inseparable. Some days would be easier than others, but often the hardest and most taxing demands were when the weather was at its unkindest.

The picture we need to imagine here is not of the croft fireside and steaming mugs of cocoa, with 'old Shep' asleep at our feet, nor the other extreme of the cold, wet collie chained to the yard kennel. We must look at the collie's lifestyle in general, for it is the careful, conscientious shepherds and breeders of yesterday who gave us our collie of today. These men revered their four-legged workmates and gave them the respect they so rightfully deserved. At the end of each working day the dogs retired to their own domain, be it a snug dry kennel, a cosy byre or a corner of a kitchen or outhouse, where they would retire to eat, sleep and clean themselves. They would not be disturbed, for just as they knew not to intrude upon or disturb the hand that fed and cared for them during *their* 'quiet time', they could be assured that when at rest humans would not disturb their peace and thinking time. Their beds would be simple; in fact, the dogs often preferred to revert to instinct and dig and

Although both strong and powerful when working sheep, a collie is still capable of being both gentle and graceful in its movements.

Bred for speed and stamina. This dog's mind is concentrating on his work while his back legs are propelling his body forwards at great speed.

dogs were educated enough not to kill the flocks they tended, but the strong survival and pack instinct taught them how to find any supplements they may be lacking. An animal at one with nature instinctively knows how and where to acquire vitamins and minerals. What is important is that the ancestral collie's way of life and living conditions may have been different from that of today's collie, but the degree of intelligence, stamina and hardiness has not lessened.

Now we have a mental picture of the collie at the turn of the century. His colour, coat and general appearance varied, but he was a rugged chap, honest, hardworking and loyal. The ancestral collie presented an economical little package capable of great stamina and intelligent enough to be able to work on his own initiative. A picture of today's collie, apart from the quality of the photography, will vary little from the hardy

burrow their own domain (today's collie when presented with a nice warm bed of human acceptability will often surprise his owner by moving bag and baggage to the most unlikely place!). Their diet would be basic – gruel, maize and meat, depending on availability, and many shepherds would make their own 'mix', adding and subtracting according to condition and work. Those dogs fed on a more meagre diet would seek their own 'supplements' by foraging, finding their own minerals and vitamins in the surrounding vegetation, just as their pack ancestors did. Fortunately, feeding has improved over the years and the choices now are many and varied but with this comes problems for the non-working collie. It is important to remember that although the diet of these ancestral collies was basic the dogs not only thrived but also had the stamina they needed for the work asked of them. An important factor is that many of these dogs were allowed the freedom to choose their own sleeping quarters and to forage. These

Rugged, honest, hard-working and loyal. Thanks to careful breeding these attributes have been passed down through generations of collies.

creature of earlier years. Far from deteriorating, his breeding, through careful thought, has improved, giving us better-sighted, more versatile collies able to turn their skills to all areas of work rather than specialize in just one aspect.

We have drawn a picture of the collie in his original environment, from pack dog to the working, shepherding collie. So does this same dog readily adapt to pet life? Should he be asked to do so? Can we overcome those strong herding instincts or should we try to eliminate them for the sake of the pet dog?

The answer cannot be simple as the collie varies widely in temperament and character. The question, 'Should these dogs be in any other than a working home?' is irrelevant – the fact is that they are, and are also capable of adapting to most situations. With the recognition of the sheepdog by the Kennel Club many changes have evolved, and the collie is now officially the Border Collie, with a popularity that means he is found in many different walks of life. This is not going to change, and so we must all work

in unity for the benefit of the breed and its intelligence. It is the intelligence, humour and versatility of the ancestral collie that handlers outside shepherding homes have seen and taken into their lives. We must not downgrade the dogs of working parents who have been labelled 'not good enough to work'. It means that they were not able to do the particular job in question (for example, not all dogs will work cattle but they may excel with sheep), were not given adequate training or were bred incorrectly. We now understand that it has taken years of careful breeding to produce this wonderful breed, but it can be weakened by careless mistakes or lack of knowledge of the genetic make-up of the ancestors. Only a foolish person blames a breed of dog for failing to come up to expectations. It is we humans who are responsible for doing 'the homework' and making sure we breed a dog worthy of his ancestors. If the ingredients of an original recipe are altered, the end product is never the same quality. Similarly, if we vary the genetics of breeding too much we may

A breed with years of history behind it. This collie waiting patiently to continue with its work is lost in its own thoughts.

have a collie who has lost his original qualities. We now have the answer to, 'Should we eliminate these instincts for the pet collie?' If we are prepared to alter the breed for the sake of easier handling we are changing the breed, a breed with years of history behind it – it's far better to understand it or view it from afar! Just as careful breeding provided us with the collie of today, similar care must be taken to ensure that our working collie can be introduced safely into most environments without losing his original qualities! Although quality rests heavily with the breeders, so too must potential owners share this responsibility. Too many collies purchased as puppies without care being taken about breeding, feeding, care and management become problem adolescents. A percentage of the problems can be genetical, but a large proportion is mismanagement, or a failure to understand the dog's requirements. The emphasis has to be on what the collie really needs to be content, and not what the human element may think he needs.

Having drawn this mental image of a special dog – the Border Collie – only you can decide whether you are ready to share your life with one. The cost, other than financial, is an extra being to consider, its welfare and how to educate it. The reward, if done correctly, is a loyal family member with both intelligence and humour.

Having discovered what a Border Collie is, the next step is where to find it.

The Border Collie as a Breed

Border Collies are strong-minded intelligent individuals. They are bred to work, and by developing the natural instincts to produce a sheepdog we have also produced a dog so versatile it is capable of adapting to other lifestyles. It is important to retain the strong natural instincts to keep the Border Collie true to its original breeding. These strong instincts, when understood and handled correctly, are the very instincts that give the collie the humour, versatility and loyalty it is renowned for.

CHAPTER 2

Finding Your Border Collie

Finding a Border Collie may not be difficult, but before you rush out and buy the first cuddly puppy you see, stop, and take a long, hard look at what you really want. For you are not just going out and looking for *a* dog, you are looking for *the* dog, one that will be a part of your life for a long time, so before you go searching try to make sure that you have an idea of what you are looking for.

You know you are looking for a particular breed, but these are very individual dogs, so you need to make sure that your choice will fit in with your lifestyle and be compatible to your requirements. So what are your requirements?

What do You Want from Your Dog?

Before you take that all-important step, why do you want a Border Collie? Do you want a family dog, a guard dog or a working dog? How much time will you be able to devote to it each day? Are all the family committed to having an extra responsibility? Will there be any children involved in the dog's life? If you live on your own, will your dog be left unattended for any length of time? Are you intending to participate in any competitions and if so what kind? Do you want a puppy or an older dog?

If you are looking for a dog for the sole reason of its being a guard dog, a Border Collie will not only take unkindly to any restrictions which may be imposed upon it, but it will also suffer if it is denied contact with its human partner. A collie will naturally protect its own if it can identify with its own 'pack' – for example, a family dog will also be protector should the occasion arise. If you are looking for a dog to work, you will need to make sure that it has breed lines which are favourable to your kind of work. For example, a herdsman looking for a dog for his cattle would be foolish to buy a dog from parents who were not strong cattle dogs.

If your dog is to be competitive, you will need to know the requirements of that particular sport. A quiet dog from shy parents may not be the best choice for agility or obedience, as not all dogs like to be noticed and not all dogs like crowds.

First of all, what have you set your heart on, a puppy or an older dog? If you feel you would like a puppy you need to know as much as possible about training *before* you bring it into your home, and you must also be sure that you are in a position to give the time needed to raise a puppy. If you are working and the house is going to be empty for a large part of each day, then it would be unfair to ask a puppy to adapt to your life when you are not really in a position to adapt to his. If you have small children or a baby, do you have the time to take on an extra responsibility? Remember that the person who is prepared to exercise the dog is not always the person who is left looking after it all day, and all members of a family must be prepared and able to look after, teach and be responsible for the puppy. You may have cats or rabbits or other pets which a puppy may try to 'hunt', so can you guarantee them a 'safe house'? However, if you do choose a puppy you will have the satisfaction of being able to train it the way you want, and you will not only have lots of fun and laughter but also some lovely memories.

If you feel that an older dog would be better for you, would you be prepared to give a 'rescue' dog a secure home, or maybe this is what you already have in mind? If you take on a rescue, you must be prepared for some possible traumatic moments and there will be times when you could be driven almost to despair, but the rehabilitation of a rescue to a secure, trusting companion has a reward which is all its own!

The 'Rescue' or Older Dog

The training of an older or problem dog will require going back to basics, which are puppy training, plenty of patience and a great deal of common sense.

It is not usually difficult to find an older dog that needs rehoming. There are various rescue organizations, some of which are dedicated to just Border Collies. If you go through rescue channels you will probably be asked to give a standard donation and, hopefully, you will have some kind of back-up service, but do check on this first. Not all the rescues are official and they may not give any help after you have taken your dog home, and, although you will be told you can take the dog back if it does not settle, most people feel they cannot subject the dog to another rejection. Most rescue organizations will be able to advise you on choosing a dog and will help you with rehabilitation, but don't be frightened to ask questions and find out as much as possible about any known history of the dog. Not all dogs in rescue are official 'rescues' – occasionally, dogs are taken into care when their owners can no longer keep them. The only problem you are likely to encounter with such a dog is loss of confidence, and that can soon be restored with plenty of Tender Loving Care. Reputable rescue organizations do a marvellous job, often depending on public support and fundraising, and many will be happy for you to spend time exercising and getting to know some of the dogs in their kennels. Dog walking can be rewarding and it may help you to make up your mind which dog is for you. Occasionally you will find an advertisement for rehoming an older dog in a local newspaper or pet shop but do be careful. Find out why the dog is to be rehomed and, unless you know the owners, don't be afraid to ask neighbours if they can give you any helpful information.

Taking on an older dog or a rescue does not necessarily mean you are taking on a problem, but you are accepting into your home an older being who will be used to a different routine and possibly a different way of life to yours. If you compare this to the difference between bringing up a baby or adopting an older child, you would know immediately that a 'settling in' period would be necessary with the older child. A time of getting to know one another, sorting out new routines and above all learning to understand each other's needs would be necessary. A dog that has been mistreated will automatically receive plenty of TLC from a loving new owner, but the dog that has previously had a loving home needs just as much consideration. Whatever reasons the previous owner had to part with their pet will be a mystery to the dog in question and, unless it already knows you, it will be confused and bewildered. Both past and present owner may have been planning the change of home for some while, but it will be new to the dog until its old 'pack leader' suddenly walks out of its life! Most dogs have a 'sixth sense' which tells them something is happening which is not a part of their normal lives. No matter how discreet and calm human beings try to be they give off certain messages which they probably know nothing about, but the dog picks them up immediately. Just because the dog has come from a good home and has had previous training does not mean extra effort will not be needed from the new owner; after all, while the words you use may be the same, the voice will be different! Take every effort to make the dog feel at home. For example, if you have its bed and any familiar blankets don't put them where *you* want, but see if the dog indicates where *it* feels safe. If you can't detect any messages think where its 'den' was in the old home and try to offer somewhere similar. It may have been used to sleeping under the stairs or in the kitchen, or if it suddenly runs from you into the conservatory or even the garden shed, don't worry, that may have been its favourite place in the old home! When the dog settles it may be happy to move to your idea of a secure haven, but for the first few weeks be prepared to put some of your ideas 'on hold' until it feels it can trust you. The time to be insistent is when the dog does something that you consider to be unacceptable in your home.

One word of caution – if you have not trained a dog before be advised against taking on a dog which has shown aggression. It is very rare for a dog to be naturally aggressive and rehabilitation is often possible, but it does need specialized knowledge and training. If you are looking at a dog from a private source and have any doubts about its temperament, think very carefully before you make your decision.

Looking for a Puppy

Well, where can you start? Initially in the local newspaper pet column, the pet shop, the telephone directory, the dog club, the dog magazines, or the local rescue centres. You could be spoiled for choice and it is so easy to fall in love with a puppy that when you have a whole litter to choose from you can be faced with a difficult decision. The puppy which you prefer most in the litter is not necessarily going to be the best choice for you. The breeder will know more about the developing characters of the puppies as individuals so don't be afraid to ask questions.

If you are going to a rescue organization for your puppy there may be little, if any, information about the parents.

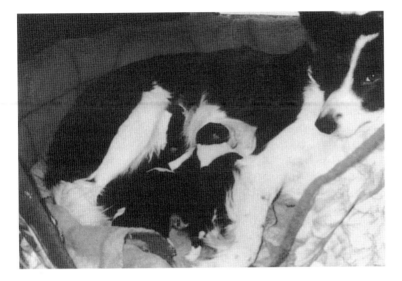

The 'milk bar' is a safe place to be while Mum watches contentedly over them. Megan has a warm bed inside to rear her puppies but her natural instinct was not satisfied until the bed was placed in a corner.

The staff may be able to give you some of the background history, why the puppies are in rescue, whether they were born there, whether any of the staff have seen the parents. If you are buying your puppy from the breeder then you should have much more information available to you, but the information which should help often causes more confusion!

To begin with, you may be quite sure you know what you are looking for – a Border Collie puppy, what could be simpler than that? You may even have a mental picture of the dog you would like and when you choose your puppy this picture may be in your mind, but there is no guarantee that the little bundle of fluff will grow up to look anything like the mental picture you have conjured up. You may also have visions of playing ball, going to shows, swimming, and any number of other activities which you hope your dog will be interested in. It may grow up to have other ideas! When you finally make the choice and feel you know which puppy you want you may not

be prepared for some of the questions the breeder may ask you. Do you want your puppy registering? It could be a KC dog or an ISDS dog or it could be dual-registered, it may have been tested for CEA and there may be no HD in the family! Now you could know exactly what all this means, or you could be left reeling.

You need to know what you want and where to find it, so if we simplify some of the terminology you will find your options lessen and this will make it easier. Don't let the word 'breeder' confuse you or lull you into a sense of false security. When you make your first enquiry about a litter of puppies and you are told you are talking to the breeder, do not assume he or she is necessarily a knowledgeable breeder. A breeder is a person who breeds puppies; *the* breeder is the person who bred the litter you are enquiring about. If further enquiries prove that the person who bred the litter is simply a breeder make sure they are a breeder of Border Collies rather than someone who breeds an entirely different dog and just happens to have one Border Collie. A registered breeder sounds good but ask exactly what this means. They may be registered with the local council as a breeder (the law changes regularly but the appropriate council department will tell you the requirements at the time), or they may be registered with one of the large societies, such as the Kennel Club or the International Sheep Dog Society. Whatever the registration, it does not automatically mean that if you choose from this litter you will be receiving all the back-up that a conscientious breeder should be giving – this is something you have to find out for yourself.

Ask if you can visit the kennels and note the immediate response to your question. If the puppies are still quite young the breeder should be cautious, as the more people visiting young puppies the greater the risk of disease. Don't be impatient if you have to wait a few weeks, or offended if you are asked to disinfect or remove shoes when visiting. Expect not to be allowed to touch very young puppies. It is better to be safe than sorry and you can go back in a few weeks for a cuddle. Some breeders will allow potential owners to look at the litter when it is young, especially if they have more customers than puppies. If someone has their heart set on a puppy with a white collar and there is not one in the litter they will want to know if that person can be taken off the list. As soon as the puppies are older you will be invited back to make your choice. There is no standard procedure and you will find that the breeders can differ greatly. They will have found what works for them, and what should concern you now

A healthy, well-matched litter tucking in to a good meal. No one is hanging back and there are no arguments.

is whether you want a puppy from the litter you are looking at.

When you do visit, take a good look at the surroundings. They don't have to be immaculate and fitted with all 'mod cons', but they should be clean and tidy with no 'danger zones' (nails, pieces of wood, deep water, and so on). The puppies should look happy and relaxed and should run to the breeder full of confidence, with coats in good condition, and, although happy puppies are not always clean puppies, there should be no old dirt, or dried, matted sections of coat or bald patches. It is inevitable that puppies will pick up little visitors on their travels around the garden and play area, but persistent scratching may indicate a parasite problem. When you see puppies with nice bright eyes, comfortable but not swollen stomachs and faces full of mischief you can begin to trust the breeder. Ask to see the mother of the litter – from any private source the mother should be available (unless a tragedy has occurred and the litter is hand-reared), and even though she has just reared a litter of puppies she should still look well. Some bitches keep good condition when they are nursing, but some spend so much time worrying about their brood that they forget to look after themselves. Although her condition may not be one hundred per cent and her coat may have suffered a little, she should still look well fed and cared for. Enquire about the stud dog (the father of the litter). It may belong to the breeder, in which case you can see both parents and spend some time with them. If the stud dog is not available find out as much as possible about it, as things like colour, coat and temperament all play an important part in a puppy's genetic make-up. Ask for a contact number for the owner of the stud dog – it may be only a short distance away or it may be at the other end of the country, but whether you intend to see it or not the breeder should be happy to give you the details. Does the breeder only have the one bitch or are there other dogs in the kennels? There may be older dogs related to the puppies that you can see, or photographs of previous puppies sent by appreciative owners. This all helps to create a picture for you of the puppies you are looking at, as well as their parents and the way they are kept. If you are shown the puppies and spared only as much time as is necessary from the breeder it is quite likely you will not get any help after you have made your purchase. If you are confused and maybe just a little bored by all the exploits the breeder tells you of their dogs, take heart that at least you know he or she is proud of them!

You will be seeking different 'information' if you are looking at puppies from a 'one-off' litter. This type of litter usually comes into the world for one of two reasons – they are the result of an accidental mating or the owner of the bitch wants to keep a puppy from her to bring up as she gets older. With the accidental mating the owner may know which is the stud dog, but it is more likely he or she didn't know there were any puppies on the way until it was too late to do

It is a bitch's natural instinct to protect her young and her wishes should be respected. This litter with two white puppies had a tri-coloured father and a black and white mother.

When choosing a puppy it is always nice to be able to see other progeny. This little family group spans five generations.

anything about it. If someone is breeding for a 'replacement', it is more than likely they will have tried to breed a nice litter of pups.

Puppies are sometimes advertised in pet shop windows and other similar sources; it is a cheaper form of advertising and attracts the attention of children. If someone is looking for a puppy it should be the result of careful forethought and not because the children are pleading. If you see a litter of puppies advertised through a media you feel you would not use if you were selling, then you may be wiser not to buy from that advertisement.

Now you have an idea of where to look, some of the things to look for and a little

of what to expect of a breeder. But what about the rest of the confusing terminology?

What is Registration?

If you looking at puppies from a rescue organization or an accidental mating the chances are registration will not be an option you can take, but if you are buying from a planned litter then registration should come into the equation.

There are two main bodies a Border Collie can be registered with, the International Sheep Dog Society (ISDS) and the Kennel Club (KC). For those who fully understand registration there is no problem, for those who are learning, the classification of the different organizations can be confusing.

Originally the only registration was with the ISDS, an organization founded in 1906, by a group of shepherds for the good of the sheep dog and its future. In 1955, after careful research of pedigrees dating back to the turn of the century, the first Stud Book was produced, followed by more research, more information and more Stud Books. These Stud Books are now a valuable reference for breeders from all over the world who are dedicated to maintaining the quality of the breed as a working dog. Each dog registered with the ISDS receives a Stud Book number and the pedigree of each registered dog can be traced by researching the books, finding the ancestors and forming a 'family tree', which is the dog's pedigree sheet. With these pedigree sheets breeders can see at a glance the ancestry of potential breeding stock and more research will give them the information needed on temperament, power and other factors to produce a compatible mating. It is this final research where modern breeding often fails – knowledge of the actual dogs in the pedigree is important and this is gained not just through the accolades of the dog but by word of mouth. No matter how many awards a dog has won or how good it may have been, if it was difficult to train, bad-tempered or blind it is not one to be used for breeding. Many of the dogs on the pedigree sheets are seen time and again and not all will have been champions, but they may have produced champions. These are 'foundation dogs', dogs which have been a part of the foundation of the modern Border Collie, with strong genes that have been passed on to their sons and daughters, producing every so often, perhaps only every ten or fifteen years, more 'foundation dogs'. So the quality is maintained and the best breed lines are all based on the same foundation stock.

The breed is registered with the ISDS as a 'Working Sheep Dog (or Border Collie)', but with the recognition of the breed by the KC the registration title of Border Collie on their register was given to dogs with proof of breeding (i.e. dogs registered with the ISDS). The title 'working sheepdog' was given to dogs with no proof of breeding. The registration title is where new owners become confused, as the KC will register dogs from ISDS or KC parents and their status is Border Collie. However, there are many sheepdogs born of parents that are not registered with either association and have no proof of breeding, which are registered with the KC as Working Sheepdogs. The pitfall here is that they are classed by many as not being pure or 'proper' Border Collies. The ISDS will only register puppies from ISDS parentage and their status on the registration card is 'Working Sheep Dog or Border Collie'. I often encounter confusion when I describe my dogs as sheepdogs (dogs which work sheep), as anyone who is only familiar with the KC definition of a Working Sheepdog immediately identifies them as not being 'pure bred', when in actual fact they are registered with the ISDS.

The term 'Border Collie' is acknowledged by both the ISDS and the KC as pure bred. A 'Working Sheepdog' is the KC 'uncertain parentage' registration. A 'Working Sheep Dog' (note the spelling) is the ISDS description of a Border Collie. A sheepdog is a dog which works sheep!

A healthy litter of pups with shiny coats and bright eyes waiting to go out to play.

Is Registration Important?

Do not underestimate the importance of registration, but make sure you are aware of what it means and that you use it to its full potential. Also, be aware that being registered does not automatically mean a puppy is well bred. It is easy to think that a puppy who is a 'registered pedigree' with champion parents is going to be a good dog, but unfortunately this does not always follow. Registration simply means that the puppy is, or is eligible for, registration with either or both of the two main bodies (KC and ISDS). Some competitions require registration status, so if you are hoping to be competitive with your dog or if you are likely to want to breed at a later date then registration becomes important. If a puppy is registered it will have a traceable pedigree and this sheet of paper

will tell you if there is any inbreeding in the line. Even if you do not fully understand the pedigree sheet you will be able to see if the same names seem to appear too often. If the parents are registered you can ask to look at their registration cards for proof of eye testing (the ISDS will tell you the current requirements for the eye testing of breeding stock). Careful breeding has put a tight control on PRA (Progressive Retinal Atrophy) and CEA (Collie Eye Anomaly) and it is the responsibility of the breeder to make sure they are breeding 'sound' stock.

If you are looking for a puppy you will be trying to make sure you make as few mistakes as possible and by listening to the advice of others you can learn a lot. Everyone has their own opinions, so you may find that some of the advice is conflicting and that some of the most confusing information for a beginner is about the 'Big Three': PRA, CEA and HD. The first two affect the eyes and you may hear differing opinions about the seriousness of these in the breed. Thanks to the eye-testing scheme, sensible breeding and the vigilance of the ISDS we no longer have the blindness problem that was consistent with the earlier sheepdogs. We now have dogs attaining old age, in some cases very old age, with sight that has suffered no impediment other than normal deterioration. Puppies can be tested at an early age for CEA but PRA does not show until later years, so it is important that all breeding stock is eye-tested and it is heartening to know that the failure rate at the time of writing is a very low percentage. A list of dogs that have failed the eye test is kept by the ISDS, so with a little effort and careful studying of breed sheets this percentage should be kept low. I honestly believe that too many breeders spend time looking for different stud dogs rather than remaining with a 'tried and tested' one. The search for breeding that 'special' dog can be the downfall of a litter if the homework has not been carefully done.

Hip Dysplasia, or to give it its full title Canine Hip Dysplasia, will also be the cause of more conflicting advice and you may be told that HD is a problem with the Border Collie as a breed. I am going to spare only a few lines in this chapter on HD as it will be covered more thoroughly in later chapters on nutrition and exercise. Hip Dysplasia is more common in the larger breeds and I don't believe it has ever been a problem with Border Collies. I will not argue that there will have been lame collies in the past and that there is probably a higher

percentage of lame ones at the present time. I doubt very much that the lame collies in the past were all X-rayed so we cannot be sure why they were lame, but if there is an increase in lameness it has come with the change of life-style. Incorrect diet and exercise can cause stress on the joints and damage to young dogs, causing hip damage. It would appear to be sensible to buy stock from parents who have a low hip score, but what about the grandparents and great-grandparents? Many dogs have been taken out of a breeding programme because of alleged bad hips, but if those dogs were of good sound breeding and

A prick-eared, medium-coated, dark-coloured collie. Its genetics, like its appearance, suggest an energetic dog.

A medium-coated collie with folded ears but a nice light brown eye (see Chapter 9). The eyes balance the ears, suggesting no less energy than the prick-eared collie but maybe a little gentler.

A short-coated, prick-eared dog with one brown and one wall-eye. Genetics suggest a lively energetic dog with a strong mind.

their hips had suffered damage we may have lost a good breeding line. In the words of a very good friend who is also a vet, "We have a duty to breed as fine a sheepdog as we can and part of that duty is being careful not to breed in any defects which are avoidable. But we also must be careful not to spend so much time breeding the perfect body that we loose the quality of the sheepdog." I could not agree more. Soundness of eye, limb and body are important and you must choose carefully from a reliable source, but try not to let politics and confusing advice prevent you from recognizing a good litter of pups.

If you buy an unregistered puppy, unless the parents are registered you will have no background information to draw on regarding eye testing or lameness and no knowledge of the temperament of the ancestors. This does not mean that an unregistered puppy is not a good puppy, but with less information the risk is higher. If you buy a registered puppy you can draw on information about the background, the genetics, any physical defects and any inbreeding. Of course, there is no guarantee that a registered puppy is going to be any better that the unregistered one, but the odds are more favourable.

Any puppy that is eligible for registration should be registered. New owners are sometimes asked if they want their puppy registering, and while their answer should be yes, it would be better if registration were automatic. It should be included in the price rather than be an optional extra. For the purpose of ISDS registration the puppy should be entered on a puppy folder and a sketch should be done. The breeder does all this but you can ask to see the sketch if it is not done when you are present. If you have received no registration card from the breeder by the time the puppy is five months old begin to take steps to find out why. When the puppy reaches six months old the registration fee has penalty costs added to it.

Choosing your Puppy

Before you go to look at a litter of puppies make sure you know what you want. You may have a mental picture of the type of dog you would like and if you want a dog for a specific purpose then appearance may be important. If you feel you would like to 'show' your dog in the 'breed' ring, then a certain criterion would be required (the Kennel Club can provide the breed standard). If you will be asking your dog to work in very muddy conditions on a regular basis, then a short-coated dog would be the obvious choice. If your dog is to be a companion then the only requirements will be your own personal ones. However, some facts may be worth considering before you decide. Genetics are complicated and can be confusing, but they do play a large part in the dog's character and the type of dog you are choosing: for example, short-coated dogs are usually more energetic than their longer-coated cousins; dogs with long droopy ears are often quite passive; dogs with pricked ears tend to be very keen and quick to learn; and short-coated prick-eared dogs need a keen, energetic owner! Blue Merles (flecked blue/grey coats) are usually very energetic and don't forget the more energy, the more wicked the sense of humour! These are just guidelines and there is always the exception to the rule, but it is worth noting that if you are not sure about training a Border Collie it may be wiser not to choose one where the odds are stacked in favour of it being a handful. Still with genetics, if the puppy has a long coat but one or both parents have short coats, the chances are the puppy may have the short-coated characteristics.

When you do look at a litter stand back and observe – they will all look as if they want to belong to you but you are only looking for one! The one which runs to the front is not 'choosing you' – there is always a leader and this little being is just checking you out. The one standing at the back may not be shy of you but may simply be respecting the puppy leader. The puppy leader will have a mind of its own and see itself in charge, so is this what you want? A quiet, shy puppy *can* be an extrovert, happy dog and the strong one *can* be taught the rules of your pack, but which one is for you? If you are positive and have a loud voice the shy one may not be a good choice, but if you are quiet and not very confident then the strong puppy may put you in your place. But you will also need to have confidence to deal with the shy puppy. It may just be a thinker and be observing you, or it may be genuinely frightened. No puppy should be frightened – it may be a result of the genetics, in which case the other puppies may not all be consistent in temperament, or the puppy may have suffered a fright. If this is the case, the breeder should have been taking measures to put this right. All puppies should trust the breeder!

Check the appearance of the puppies, make sure none are lame and check their mouths – one jaw should not be longer than the other, as overshot puppies may have difficulty eating. The best of breeders can produce the occasional puppy with an uneven jaw, just as they may have a white puppy in a litter, or one short-coated one. It is not a major fault if it is only slight, which it will be if it is the result of a throwback. If it is the result of inbreeding, then it will probably be very obvious and the whole litter should be regarded as suspect as a result of poor quality breeding.

Whichever puppy you choose, from the moment it enters your heart and your home it is yours, and the rest of the litter and any mental picture you may have had will cease to exist. Your picture is now a reality.

Choosing Your Puppy with Care

First make sure you are in a position to take on the responsibility of a Border Collie. Don't rush out and buy the first puppy you see, the characters are so varied that you need to do some research into the kind of life your dog will lead with you and the kind of life the puppy you are looking at will need. The puppy's needs must be taken into consideration. Make the time and effort needed to check the background of both the breeder and the puppy's ancestors. Cutting corners may save time but it can cost you a lot more in the long run!

CHAPTER 3

Taking Your Puppy Home

You will have waited a long time for the day you can collect your puppy and take it home – after weeks or maybe months of careful planning and forethought, at last it is a part of your life. A fluffy little bundle of fun that could not possibly take over the household, after all it is only tiny and looks so angelic! But what happens when this little angel begins to develop its own ideas as to who is in charge, how to behave and how to devour a carpet in one easy lesson? It doesn't happen overnight but is a slow progression, gradually creeping up on you until suddenly you are confronted with a four-legged adolescent who seems to believe human beings are there for its amusement. Prevention is better than cure! Training begins from day one, but the preparation for it begins far sooner.

Before you bring your puppy home decide where it is going to live. It needs a place of its own where it can feel safe and secure and where any visitors will not be able to disturb it. You may have a recess under the stairs, or a large kitchen or hall with a 'free' corner, but wherever you choose for your puppy it needs to be a 'happy' place.

A puppy coming into your home brings its own little supply of extra baggage, for almost like a new baby it is going to be demanding of both your time and attention. When it enters your home your puppy has just left its own family (its pack) and a familiar routine, and it will change from being one of a litter to the centre of attention. This is a big upheaval and you will be doing everything possible to help the puppy to settle, but after the first few days you will inevitably start to revert back to your more normal routine. Your puppy is now facing another upheaval, for it will no longer always be the centre of attention and it will have more free time which it may use for making mischief.

Choosing a Bed

There are many different kinds of dog beds, but I strongly advise buying or making something into which you can fasten your puppy. Collapsible cages are popular for they can be dismantled, are light to carry, and take up little room when folded. Alternatively, the plastic 'kennels', specially designed for transporting small animals, are easy to keep clean, have a wire door, and the solid sides offer privacy for the dog in its own 'space'. If you are handy at DIY you may be able to make a perfectly good box with a door and all mod cons for your dog, and at little expense, but wood is not easy to keep clean and you may find that smells linger. Remember, when you are buying a dog bed you have to think about what the dog needs and not what you think it might need. Your puppy has just left the safety of its mother and a familiar pen; it may have been in a house or a kennel or a farm barn but this is all it has known and it has felt secure there. It will have spent its resting time snuggled up to 'Mum' in as small a space as she could provide. It would have felt safe here and if at any time it was unsure it would have been to this space and 'Mum' where it would have gone. If you substitute this safety for an open bed the small puppy is vulnerable, as it has no protective 'boundary' around it, and as it grows in both size and confidence it may 'remove' to a place of its own choosing. If you provide your puppy (or older dog) with a place of its own you will begin

to establish your 'house' rules immediately and in a way which a dog can understand.

When you have chosen your dog bed make sure you have a good supply of bedding. This can be pieces of old blanket, quilt or special pet bedding, the latter being easy to wash and dry. There are some excellent fur beds available which will fit in a cage or a plastic bed or can be used on their own. Most importantly, make sure that on the day you fetch your puppy home you have something warm and snug for it to nestle into. Straight from its mother, bewildered and unsure, it will want to feel secure and safe whether it is in a box or on someone's knee it will soon hide itself in the warm furry bedding. It may see several different humans and receive plenty of love and affection but if it always has this little bit of comfort to relate to and to identify with its leader then safety is always close at hand. The

Your puppy will have spent its time snuggled up to Mum in as small a space as she could provide. Meg preferred to be allowed to make her own 'safe' area for her family and always chose a snug little corner.

A blanket or a fur bed used in a cage can be transferred to any part of the house and your puppy will recognize it as his 'own room'. This little chap is as content and snug in his bed as he was with his Mum.

newcomer to your life may initially be nervous and shy or it may want to investigate, but exhaustion will soon take over and it will fall asleep. Wherever it falls asleep place it gently in its box on the soft bedding and close the door.

You can now begin to establish some boundaries in a way that makes your puppy not only feel safe, but which it will also find to be fun. The beauty of a 'mobile' dog home is that you can take it anywhere and it offers instant security to its occupant, but it must be a 'happy' home and must not be used as a punishment. Spend the first day at home getting to know your puppy, making sure the kennel is close at hand. If the puppy does not go in voluntarily to sleep, lift it gently in each time it has fallen asleep and close the door. Be there when it wakes up to greet it and invite it back into your 'kennel', and in a short while you will have a puppy who will automatically seek out its pen or bed when it is tired.

You make the house rules but if your puppy is allowed to climb on the furniture, as an adult he will see nothing wrong in settling down there with muddy paws.

Spend time with your puppy on the floor rather than lifting him onto the furniture and he will grow into a confident adult knowing his boundaries.

Always make sure that your puppy has something in its bed to keep it amused. It may be something to chew or play with, and if you have invested in a standard portable kennel it will have a small water bowl attached to it so it need never be thirsty. Encourage your puppy to spend time in its own little home and get it used to being in with the door closed for short periods of time. There is nothing more frustrating than leaving a puppy in the house for a short period of time and returning to mess and destruction! The owner is unhappy, the puppy is upset and before long going out ceases to be a pleasure. If the puppy is safely fastened in its bed, there will be no damage to the owner's 'kennel' and both will be pleased to see each other. However, bear in mind that no puppy should be left on its own for long periods of time either in a pen or loose in the house. If you have to leave the house for longer than the average sleeping time of the puppy, arrange for someone to attend to its needs or take it with you in its 'kennel'.

You now have a base for your foundation training, and all training needs a strong foundation. Consider that if you were building a house and its foundation was weak, you would be limited to the size of the property and any flaws may be irreparable; you may even have to begin again! If you start with a solid foundation, any problems which may occur can soon be rectified and you need not be limited by being unable to extend the property. It is important to organize your schedule to enable you to have the time needed to build a good foundation for your puppy's training; time spent now can help to prevent so many problems when your puppy reaches adolescence.

House Rules

It really doesn't matter what rules anyone else has for their dog, this is *your* dog and if some of your rules are not approved of by others, don't worry. After all, you want to enjoy your dog and you want to enjoy it *your* way, but you must have rules and you must make sure your dog understands who is the leader. You must be consistent. For example, if your furniture is to be replaced and your dog will not be allowed on the new furniture, then it would be unfair to allow him on the old. A new armchair positioned in exactly the same place as the old one constitutes the same 'bed' to the dog that it has always been allowed to sleep on. Changing the rules for no apparent reason will cause your dog to question your reliability as a pack leader.

Very few puppies are naturally dirty – it is not in the best interest of any self-respecting bitch to allow her offspring to foul the bed, as she has to sleep in it! She will have taught the youngsters to keep their own personal area clean. On a farm it will have been easy for them to arrange their own toilet facilities, but if they were reared indoors they may have been introduced to a more domestic arrangement. Paper, sand and sawdust are all methods which are often used to encourage the puppies to go in just one area, but you need to think very carefully before you decide how to train your puppy not to soil your best carpet! With the best will in the world and the most willing of puppies you are still going to have accidents, as puppies drink a lot and only have small bladders. You therefore need to provide gentle, consistent education and a foolproof (or smell proof) emergency area. While you are busy trying to teach your puppy to use the 'great outdoors' to relieve himself, make sure you explain to him just what area he can use. As a tiny being he will only be leaving you tiny 'presents', but if he is led to believe he can leave them anywhere as long as it is

outside it may not be very pleasant when he is an adult dog.

If you have a garden that contains flowerbeds for which you have a strong affection, make sure you offer some protection for them while junior is still learning his boundaries. If possible, provide an area for digging and playing and if there are children to consider try to provide a 'child-free' area. In an ideal world both children and dogs should have a 'recluse' area, a space to which each can retire in the knowledge that they will not be disturbed by the other. If space is limited I would recommend that preference be given to the dog. If this area is in the form of a pen or run the puppy or adult dog can retire there without fear of being pestered. Remember that while your own children may adhere to your 'dog rules', other children may not, and your dog should be able to have a 'safety zone'.

There will be certain items you will need to buy before your puppy arrives, but they do not need to be expensive and in some cases you can adapt. If your dog is going to be accompanying you in the car regularly it may well be worth you investing in the 'portable' crate or cage, which will provide it with an excellent mobile home. Toys are not essential and in many cases they provide far more entertainment for the humans than for the dogs. Once again you can improvise, but be careful you do not provide a mistake. Do not give an old shoe, sock, towel, duster or anything else which the puppy could recognize elsewhere – it can hardly be blamed for chewing your best shoe if you give it an old one to play with. Remember that it doesn't see things the way humans do, so we have to look at life from the puppy's viewpoint. For the first few days you need not worry

If you give your puppy toys and don't object to him chewing them, you cannot blame him when he adds your prized possessions to his list of amusements.

Laying the Foundation for Training

A good bed in the form of a cage or box is essential to early training, but don't provide a variety of toys as they are not needed. Make sure you have some basic rules ready to apply in the first few days and think very carefully before you choose a method of toilet training. Dogs do not understand human language, but they understand body language and can associate sound to actions. If you take the time to explain to your puppy what it should do rather than expect it to mind-read, good manners will become second nature. Consider the first few days to be the first bricks in the foundation of training.

---

about keeping your new puppy entertained, and as the first few weeks pass you will know what kind of toys to provide and what games to play. However, to begin with concentrate more on getting your little four-legged friend to focus on you and not a myriad of toys, titbits and playthings.

You are now laying the first few bricks of your foundation, and if you build with care you will be starting to create that special partnership that the Border Collie is so willing to be a part of.

Early Training and Good Manners

I am often asked, 'At what age should a collie be trained?' My reply is always the same: 'At what age do you begin to teach children good manners?' I believe there is a misconception regarding training Border Collies, for many owners who have come to me with problem dogs have been given to understand that they should not begin to train their dog until it is at least six months old. Further investigation usually reveals that this information came from a shepherd or farmer who would not begin to train a dog for sheep work until it was between at least six and twelve months old. That same dog, however, would have been taught the basics of good behaviour and good manners from the start. Good manners from your dog should be one of your first concerns, for with good manners comes respect and with respect comes good manners!

Early training is all about respect and begins on day one. There should never be the need to sit down and think 'tomorrow I must begin to train my dog'; unless you are training for something specific such as competition work, the basics should be an ongoing process. If we think of growing up in human terms, children go to school to begin serious education and as they mature they will seek further education for the line of work they are interested in pursuing. But before they attend their first school they will have been educated with good manners, and will know their physical and mental boundaries.

The mental and physical boundaries for a dog are just as essential as those for a child and need to be established at an early age, or in the case of the older or rescue dog as soon as possible. It is a mistake to think that a puppy need not be given sensible guidelines, believing it to be too young to understand, as before weaning that same puppy will have had some sharp lessons in behaviour from its mother and it will have responded by listening and learning. A human failing is to interpret a dog's needs according to what they think they should be and not in a way that the dog will find easier to understand. The way of the pack requires the human to 'think dog'.

We have already prepared the way for a solid foundation – all that is needed now is to present it in a way which a dog will understand.

Through a Puppy's Eyes

So here it is, this little bundle of fun that is about to turn your life upside down and teach you all about a sense of humour you never knew existed! One thing I can promise you, your new puppy will soon have worked out how to control you if you do not try very hard to keep one jump in front of it. While you were wondering whether early training is really so important your puppy may have already issued you with a few choice commands and, being a nice human, you will probably have obeyed, first time! A Border Collie puppy comes complete with its basic instincts and already Mum will have begun the teaching of 'pack law', so your pup is one jump in front of you when it comes to how a pack dog should behave. It is up to you to establish your own rules, but if you do not explain your requirements in a way your puppy can understand you cannot expect pack harmony.

Toilet Training

To understand how to establish leadership in a way the puppy will readily accept, let us look at those first few, very important, hours when he is welcomed into your hearts and your home. Everything will be new and strange, the first car journey, unfamiliar humans, no familiar surroundings and no litter mates or Mum to run to, but whether nosy or nervous it will only be a short time before the puppy needs to empty his tiny

A little bundle of mischievous fun, always curious to find out what is on the other side. For their own security puppies need to know their boundaries.

is acceptable, and the second will both confuse and alarm him.

You need to choose a method of toilet training which is acceptable to you and easy for your puppy to understand, so maybe it will help if we look at possible methods and the way the puppy may view them. To begin with, where was the puppy born? If it started life on a farm it may be used to hay, straw, grass and soil, whereas a puppy born in a house may be used to paper or old towels. A breeder may use paper, sawdust, shredded paper or one of the commercial beddings for puppies. The farm puppy is about to experience quite a culture shock when it enters a house and finds no hay or straw. A puppy used to paper or cloth will not endear itself in the first few hours in its new home if it soils the family's newspaper or towels, and of course the best way for the puppy to acquire shredded paper is to shred it itself! Your response to any 'accidents' should also be logical from the puppy's point of view. It will have its own little routine, Mum will have taught it all about cleanliness and you can bet she never picked it up and rubbed its nose in it! Just imagine what a puppy may think if it searches for what *it* thinks is an acceptable place and proudly does a nice large puddle when suddenly it is picked up, turned round and has its nose firmly pushed into its own puddle. The same human responsible for this action will then probably spend the rest of the dog's life telling it off for sniffing other similar puddles! If I put myself in the dog's place I fail to see the sense in this action.

The new puppy is going to undergo changes, so make sure you provide the rules to live by now so that you are not changing the pup's habits again weeks or

bladder. Even at this early age, communication is there for you to see. He will put his nose to the ground, sniff and look for somewhere suitable; you will need to be observant as this will all happen in the winking of an eye. However, whether you read the signs quickly enough is not as important as the way you address the situation and the method of house training you have chosen. It is a mistake to ignore the first few 'puddles' and an even bigger mistake to scoop up your puppy in an effort to try and hold off the inevitable – the first will lead him to believe this months later. You are not going to have hay, straw, shredded paper or sawdust over your floors and if you are going to provide paper, what will be your reaction if your puppy jumps on the settee and wets the Sunday papers, believing it is pleasing you! Although it is favourable to provide the puppy with as much familiarity as possible to help it to feel safe and secure in its new home, it is not wise to encourage something that will not be acceptable in the home at a later date. A puppy learns quickly if it is taught simply and one of the best methods I have found is to provide a 'litter tray'. If you rely on paper, the smell will always linger on the floor and when the puppy is old enough not to need to use an 'indoor toilet', the original area will remain a weak spot. He will not be able to understand why removing the paper means the floor is out of bounds! By using a litter tray you can put in it a substance not normally found in the house – my choice would be soil, turf or even cat litter. You can move the tray and there will be no lingering smell,

the puppy will get used to looking for the tray each time, searching for its own mark, and if you keep it near the door it will not be difficult to educate your puppy to use it outside. If you have used an 'outside' substance such as soil or turf it will be automatic for the puppy to search further afield outside and find its own private area.

Now is the time for you to begin your first 'word association' lessons. At this early age your puppy will be going to the toilet at regular intervals, so try to gauge the intervals and suggest to him by word and by showing him the area provided (inside or out) that he relieves himself. Most puppies need to relieve themselves after a meal, so you can begin straight away to familiarize him with whatever command you want him to understand. If you are consistent and teach your puppy exactly what is required of him it will take only a few short lessons for him to be not only clean in the house but also to have his own area outside. If you have provided him with a word to associate

A puppy needs a home of his own, he will not only feel secure he will have more respect for your 'home'.

with his toilet he will not be worried about displeasing you when you take him away from his familiar surroundings.

Natural Instincts in the Home

So on day one you have begun gently to show your puppy what is expected of him as regards cleanliness, but what about the kennel? You may think there is no kennel involved for your puppy, as he is living in the house and therefore doesn't need a kennel. But that is not the way the youngster will see it. He has to have a home, a den or a kennel, whatever we choose to call it – he needs it and if you don't explain what and where his home is, he will just assume he is sharing yours! So, you don't really mind that, after all he's the family dog and you want him to have the run of the house, or maybe just a portion of it. But what does the dog think?

The dog in its natural habitat would be sleeping in a small, confined 'den', large enough to be comfortable, small enough to be warm and protected. He would own that home, all its possessions (offspring) would be in it and he would be constantly on guard for predators. Outside the 'den' would be an area belonging to other pack members, an area to be protected but not the sole responsibility of the individual. If at any time the individual's den or the pack's 'area' were threatened they would fight (if forced) or, if safety were no longer guaranteed, they would move to another area. This is the lifestyle of the pack dog and the modern dog owner may not feel it applies to their dog, but old habits die hard! If we look at ourselves, the human race, through the ages we have followed certain instincts. We grow up following in the footsteps of our elders, learning

from them the basics of everyday living. We play, learn to work (hunt) and eventually we mate, producing a family and become members of the local community, conforming to its rules. Rebels are dealt with according to the rules of the society. We are aware that rebels can make our society uncomfortable to live in and we feel the need to protect both our families and ourselves, but we also know we must leave the final punishment to our leaders. Our basic instincts and those of our dogs are very similar, but unfortunately for the dogs we do not always allow for their instincts, causing them confusion.

If we look carefully at what we now know about the dog's instincts we will realize that in order for the dog to feel secure, it needs its own 'den', which it will guard in addition to the pack 'area'. It will also deal with rebels and will administer punishment if it is a leader. A human being needs to provide a 'den'

Kim and Cap watch the antics of humans with amusement, they know no one will 'invade' their private quarters so they are content to sit and watch, obviously puzzled but safe.

Rule of admission – Andrea Little asks her puppy Twix to wait a moment before being invited into her home.

for the dog to feel safe and secure, and must make it very clear what area belongs to the dog and what is the pack leader's (human's) and must establish leadership for the dog to leave management of any rebels to them.

There are many different opinions and theories on 'pack law', and I know of trainers who believe the dog should own nothing, not even their bed, and advising owners to stand in the dog's bed each day for a few moments. The theory behind this is that the dog will then not obstruct any child trying to gain admission to the bed. However, if pack law is followed correctly and the human is the leader, gaining the dog's respect and promising it safety (as a good pack leader should), the situation should not arise where a child can invade the dog's territory. If a lapse in security should occur the dog will respect the leadership of hierarchy and wait for the said leader to resolve the problem. If this sounds complicated or difficult, reverse the situation – few people will allow their dog to invade their child's privacy or to climb into their child's bed. It is amazing how some dogs prove a 'problem' for their owners, dig-

ging gardens, pinching children's toys and being generally bad mannered, yet these same dogs are fully aware of certain 'taboo' areas such as beds, bedrooms and best rooms. The owners persevered with certain rules while allowing others to lapse, or did not make them clear enough to begin with!

The cage, crate or box bed are the easiest ways of providing a safe 'den' for a puppy and also assist in teaching the puppy who owns what. You own the house, the dog owns its bed, and, yes, I do believe the dog should own its bed – otherwise, can it feel safe in something which does not belong to it? If you strip the dog of owning its bed it will take over ownership of something else; the kitchen, hall, garden or car are all there to be owned if you do not make your rules clear. If you succeed in stripping your dog of everything, leaving it owning nothing, you will face the repercussions of a dog with no pride. Such a dog may be nervous, aggressive, unsure, or just plain unhappy.

When you place your puppy carefully in its bed to sleep you are giving it a safe area, its own den. If you have done the

Andrea and Twix spend a few seconds of 'quality time' together. The first few seconds out of the cage are the most important, a puppy should focus on its owner and not immediate freedom. One minute is not very long but can make house training so much easier.

groundwork correctly to begin with it will be tired, maybe even already asleep, when you put it to bed and there will be no protest from it. When it wakes up all you have to do is to apply the rule of admission – open the door, place your hand gently on your puppy to prevent it rushing out, tell it to wait, count to five and then invite the puppy into 'your house'. Number one rule of dog training – if it sounds too simple and too easy, it is probably just plain common sense!

You are now on your way to teaching your puppy who owns what. Make sure you follow the 'please wait to enter my house' rule each time, and then prepare to teach your youngster all about chewing, toys, recall, lead walking and how to be a lovable, obedient family (pack) member.

Providing Your Puppy with a 'Safe Den'

Don't expect your puppy to try to become a human being – it only understands its own instincts. In order for you to be able to communicate you have to try to understand how it sees the world and how it would expect its pack leader to behave. Provide a 'safe den' for your puppy and make it clear that its den belongs to it and your house belongs to you. If you take away your puppy's right to own its bed you take away all its rights. A Border Collie is a proud dog and should not be stripped of its dignity!

CHAPTER 4

Common-sense Dog Training

The basics of good manners are now being established in the young dog's mind, but what about how to behave outside its den? Has the unsuspecting owner done all that is possible to make sure the puppy is kept amused; are there plenty of toys, things to chew and to tug? If so, the owner is probably playing right into the puppy's paws! Most dogs are clever, and Border Collies are both clever and manipulative. If you make sure your rules are clear they will follow them; if you are the leader they will respect you. If you fail to make your mark, believe me the collie will waste little time before it has your life organized for you!

Don't allow yourself to be mesmerized by the array of toys and 'essentials' for dogs and puppies to be found in the pet stores – before you buy anything, think very carefully.

'Think Dog'

The last thing anyone wants is a puppy chewing shoes, so why buy a 'chewy' replica? Anything that resembles something which can be found in the home is not advisable, for unless you think you can explain the difference to your puppy you could be asking for trouble. For the same reason, do not be tempted to give your puppy old socks, trainers, brushes or anything else which you will be annoyed about when it selects a newer version of the old model! It does not make 'dog sense' to disregard the chewing of kitchen units or the three-piece suite because you will be replacing them with new when the puppy is older. What it does as a puppy, it can do as an adult! Just because it has lost the inclination to chew does not mean it has developed good manners or that it now respects your furniture; it just means it no longer feels like eating it!

A puppy would not have been allowed to ruin its mother's den or the pack's area, so there is no reason for it to demolish your home, but you must make sure you explain why this behaviour is unacceptable. Prevention is better than cure and the puppy's den is the key to your home remaining in one piece. You have already established that the kennel (den) belongs to the puppy and the house to the humans, and if you have explained this simply with the 'invitation into your home' method then your puppy will already be in respect of your 'kennel'. To begin with, you must decide what you are going to allow your pup to chew; after all he is a dog, and good teeth are essential to a dog's survival. Whatever you decide on, make sure it is practical and something a dog will not have difficulty in relating to – a bone would be the natural choice and cannot be confused with any household items. Make it clear that the chewing area is the 'den' and it is not acceptable in the early stages to chew in *your* home. Think about it from the dog's point of view – if you fail to make it clear what it is allowed to chew and you do not complain when it chews its toys, there is little point in complaining when it chews your toys! How are you going to explain to your dog that all the toys on the floor which have been purchased from the pet shop are chewable? But the other toys – shoes, socks, bags, bottom shelf books,

and so on are yours and must not be chewed. Very confusing for a dog!

After the first few days of settling into the new surroundings life becomes very exciting for a young puppy, so if you do not guide it you may find it has made its own decisions about how to behave and what to chew. You are not able to sit it down and have a conversation with it and it cannot read, so a book of rules would be no good; you have to find another way of communication. When training Border Collies I have always been flexible on certain matters, they have a super sense of humour and this makes living with them such fun, but when it comes to rules which are essential, and to manners which are important, I do not negotiate.

Sandra Griffiths' Poppy sees its cage as its own private quarters and will spend 'thinking time' there knowing it will not be disturbed. As a puppy matures the use of the cage door becomes unnecessary.

I do not want my puppy to chew my house or its contents so I do not allow chewing in my house. Keep your method of teaching simple – when your puppy chews anything other than the item or bone which you have provided for chewing tell it a firm 'No', replace the non-chewing item with the chewing item and put both it and the pup back in the den. The message you are conveying is short and to the point. You only chew 'this' and you only chew it in 'there'. If the puppy comes out of its bed without the chewy item, don't worry; if it tries to chew something else repeat the same procedure. If it brings the chewy item out of the bed, put both it and the puppy back in. All the time you are gentle, firm and are talking to your puppy, getting it used to the words you want it to recognize. Imagine going out for a short while and coming back to dirty floors, chewed furniture and your books and papers all over the floor. You would not be very pleased with your little bundle of mischief and, sensing your displeasure, it would not be a happy chappie! But with this calm, controlled way of communicating with your pup, you will have nice clean floors, nothing chewed and nothing out of place; you will be able to invite your pup into your home and it will be overjoyed to see you. It takes very few days of this kind of communication for you to have established some basic ground rules, and for your puppy automatically to go into its bed without any need for the door being shut.

Toys

Humans have toys, understand them and know what they are for. Toys are for playing with, they keep us amused and they can be educational; in fact, most children's toys are dual purpose in that they teach and amuse. So what do we wish to teach a puppy with the toys that are on offer, for example what is a tuggy toy going to encourage a puppy to do? The correct way to use a tuggy toy, supposedly, is for the human to both start and finish the game. But why use one at all? In the wild, dogs will play tuggy with their elders as part of learning how to survive, how to catch the prey. In our domestic world there is no point in arousing an instinct which is not needed. A collie on a farm is never encouraged to use its teeth for anything other than eating or chewing bones, and the hysteria which often arises from a game of tug is neither natural nor necessary. If you watch a litter of puppies playing, one will often pick up a piece of cloth or wood and run around with it in its mouth, tempting the rest of the litter to challenge it for possession. A rough and tumble game of tug, and often a fight, will ensue, with the victor marching off with the prize. Modern dog is derived from the wolf and the Border Collie has retained many of the predator's characteristics, which man has channelled to produce the epitome of the working dog able to hunt, herd and stalk in order to assist the shepherd while remaining gentle and soft-mouthed. These puppies are partaking in natural educational games, learning to hunt, to be a predator and able to show aggression. However, the latter is not something we need in either a work dog or a pet. If this game needs to be introduced for a reason, for example preparing for 'manwork' or a discipline, then the trainer will know how to introduce it and at what age. I can see no reason for a pet

Puppies playing will fight over and tug a 'possession' and the victor will march off with the prize. This is natural development for a litter of puppies but arouses instincts that should not be introduced into the domestic home.

dog to engage in a game which is not of benefit to it and is not needed. If a puppy has been allowed to chew and to tug and at a later date it sees a child with a similar toy, making actions to those it identifies with the game, it may try to take possession of this toy and will see no harm in being forceful. A child does not have the reactions of an adult and the results could be unhappy.

Border Collies have sensitive hearing and quite often a squeaky toy can be annoying to them; on the other hand, if the noise does not bother your dog, then it will probably have hours of fun keeping itself amused and annoying you. This toy can have its drawbacks, as squeaking is induced by the dog biting and nipping at the toy and the constant squeaking can induce hysteria in a young puppy or dog which can lead to chewing. To avoid hysteria, the toy can be used to teach the dog to be 'gentle' and 'quiet' and to

'squeak to command', all part of education! A ball with a bell in it serves a dual purpose and the dog does not need to nip to obtain the sound. In fact, some dogs devise clever ways of making the bell ring, such as dropping the ball downstairs, or bouncing and rolling it; these are all a sign that the dog is thinking rather than acting on impulse. Whatever you choose, try to make sure that your dog is encouraged to think. It needs to use its brain so make sure it is occupied with education rather than with plotting ways to score points against you! A puppy or an adult dog with both its body and its brain correctly exercised will be content to rest when your attention is needed elsewhere, so whatever time you spend with your dog make sure it is 'quality time'. Use yourself to occupy your puppy rather than toys, and don't fall into the trap of using toys as a substitute for your attention.

Dogs communicate with body language. Gemma has found something interesting and Hope is curious, the set of his tail and his body are inquisitively tense.

Hope's body has stiffened and his tail position has altered. He would like to take the matter further but Gemma is protecting her 'find' and her body language is threateningly defensive.

Communication

At this stage, you have should have a good solid foundation for your training. Whether you have a puppy or an older dog, you need to establish your rules at the beginning and you need something solid to build on. Puppies do not come with a dictionary, they do not understand the human language and they cannot read our minds, but they can communicate by body language and they are quick to learn! As a race we are clever enough to learn different languages when the need arises, yet we often fail to make any attempt at all to understand the language of DOG! A dog is *not* exceptionally clever because it knows when you are putting on your walking shoes, going to pick up the lead or the car keys, or you are about to make a bedtime drink, but it *is* clever enough to have studied and learnt your body language.

How much of the language of the dog do we take time to study?

Body Language

It is not difficult to understand the basics of the 'dog's language'. We soon learn to 'read' when a puppy is tired, hungry, thirsty or needs to go out. These actions are easy to understand and we need to know them, but in fact our dogs never stop talking to us and quite often we are guilty of just not listening to what they have to say!

Forming a partnership with a dog requires an understanding and a bonding similar to the parent and child relationship. With the understanding of another comes the automatic knowledge of knowing how that other being is feeling and how they will respond to certain situations. Many handlers who have discussed their 'dog' problems with me spend more

Hope's body language makes it quite clear that although there is something he cannot understand he is trying very hard to 'read' human language.

Quality time is essential for any partnership. It is a time of learning and of communication. The author and young Jay share a private moment and Jay communicates in a way reserved only for her best friend.

time with their dogs than I am able to spend with mine, yet I have a better relationship with mine than they enjoy with theirs. Whatever time I have, I always make sure I spend some quality time with my dogs, whereas the owner who spends most of the day with their dog probably does not really spend much actual *time* with it. For example, a two-hour walk in which the dog is 'doing its own thing', chasing rabbits, running around like a headless chicken and checking out all the local scents, is not as companionable or as constructive as a walk lasting only half an hour but which is spent talking and listening to the dog and learning to understand it. Old dogs can still teach us something on a walk if we take the trouble to 'converse' with them.

Quality time will give the owner the opportunity to learn their dog's own language and the time spent with a new puppy is invaluable, but as the puppy grows the time spent with it is often less yet the young dog's vocabulary is growing. If you listen to your dog it will tell you which toy it prefers by the frequent use of it, but it will also look at that toy before it selects it. If you ask your dog to sit in its bed you will know by the look on its face if it is going to go straight there, or if it intends to stretch your patience. If you are playing with a dog it will tell you when the game has gone too far. Do you listen? Imagine children playing in the garden and how many times an understanding Mum may be heard to say, 'They are getting tired. If I

A friendly tail raised into a gentle wag. Malcolm Merone's Floss shows an inquisitive and amiable body language.

A 'dead' or thinking tail shows the dog's mind is working even though the body is still.

don't stop them this game is going to end in tears'? Dogs, especially puppies, can react just the same way as children – all appears well but the tail may be flying too much, they may be yapping, the eyes will be large and excited and panting will be excessive. At the end of this game, the dog will be exhausted and may even have taken to nipping. This is not a pleasant or sensible tiredness and can even lead to damage of joints and tendons. No young dog should be asked to jump or twist its body unnecessarily or to work to exhaustion point.

What's in a Tail?

The tail is an important part of a dog's conversation, but once again you need to know your dog to be able to read the signs. Tail wagging shows obvious pleasure, but not all 'tail wags' are the same. A dog greeting a friendly human will display a slightly different tail wag to the one with which it greets a friendly dog,

and the stiff 'tail wag', with head erect, when meeting a strange dog is entirely different again. Dogs will even bark at a knock on the door and wag their tail at the same time, but it will be a different wag with a different message. The

A tail between the legs is not always just a sign of fear. It can be nervousness, misunderstanding, or a sign of apprehension towards someone.

This dog is telling its handler it is issuing a challenge, its body is erect, its tail is carried high and stiff and the spinal hair is lifting slightly.

It is now evident who the dog was challenging and although his tail is still erect his body is slightly less hostile because the other dog has turned away and not accepted the challenge. Had there not been a barrier the second dog would have had to turn away sooner or accept the challenge.

messages that are misread the most are the conversations the dog has with its tail down! Many people are concerned when they see a Border Collie with its tail down, preferring to see what is referred to in many circles as a 'gay tail', one which is carried high. In the days of old and in many of the shepherding circles today, a dog with a 'dead tail' (one which hangs straight down) is worth more money than one with a 'gay tail', which most shepherds will stay away from. The tail down is a dog in 'thinking position'. Watch your dog when you are playing and if you stop the game for a moment, don't move or say anything, the dog's tail will lower while it tries to work out what you are going to do next! A dog that flies its tail continually is spending little time using its brain, whereas a dog which lowers its tail and works things out is a dog educated to think! The tail tucked inbetween the legs and the body in submissive or cowering position is the unhappy dog, but the dog who hangs its tail is probably saying to you, 'Now let me work this out!' Tails are also used for balance, so a dog running or jumping will be using its tail for an entirely different function. A tail which is set too high (a breeding fault) will not be as well equipped to run and turn at speed as the dog with the lower-set tail, an important factor in the sheepdog.

Study your puppy's body language, try to read its next movement or intention and, working on prevention being better than cure, if it is about to break the rules try to prevent it! For example, a puppy asked to wait before it takes its food will tell you if it is going to ignore you. It may only be a split second of communication, but it will be there – a quick glance at the dish, a wriggle of the back,

or a defiant pushing forward of the body. As simple and quick as the communication may be, a reaction from you to remind the puppy it has been told to do something and must adhere to rules will save much confusion and reprimanding later.

Puppy Lessons

Whatever you have planned for your dog, whether you hope it is going to be a Champion or simply the best companion you have ever had, it won't happen if you don't have some control. All dogs should be good-mannered and manners mean the basics – coming back on the first recall, staying when told to and walking sensibly on a lead. These three basics are the foundation for any other training or commands you may wish to teach. Don't let anyone brainwash you into believing you must adhere to certain rules – your dog does not *have* to sit, lie down, do 'sit stays' and 'down stays'. This is *your* dog and you make the rules, the only criteria being that the rules are sensible. Not all collies take kindly to sitting, preferring to lie down, and some may even find standing more acceptable whereas some will sit quite willingly. In the early stages you are concerned with making your puppy biddable and this can be fun if you combine it with getting to know each other.

Don't wait for your puppy to be six months old and wayward before you teach it a recall. This command is easy to teach and is good fun, but it is also essential that it be obeyed. An adult or adolescent dog with a poor recall is a menace; it will pester other dogs and people, chase rabbits and will run the risk of being run over or causing an accident. Recall is not an option – it is mandatory!

Each time your puppy runs towards you give a recall. This command does not have to be any particular word or phrase, but it must be something you are comfortable with. I usually try to stay away from words which can be confused or which sound like other commands. My recall is the standard shepherd's 'That'll do'. Most of the shepherd's commands are lyrical and this appeals to the dog's hearing, making it easier to teach. The command used in most training classes is 'here' or 'come', prefixed by the dogs name, but I have to question what is the recall – the name or the command? Most dogs know when you are talking to them, so really the only time when you need to use their name is if you have several dogs in your presence, and even then unless they are your dogs you would not be addressing them. I know when my children were little I did not have to use their names at the beginning of each sentence and I believe that when a dog constantly hears 'Fido come' then its name becomes a command and ceases to be a name. Perhaps if the command has two syllables the temptation to use the name out of context would not be so great, for example 'come here' or 'to me', only using the name when it is necessary to get the dog's attention. A dog with its attention on you should only need a recall, but a young dog with its attention fixed elsewhere can be addressed by its name to gain its attention and then given its recall. It is a simple method but it gains the young dog's attention and encourages it to listen to the following command, thus avoiding disobedience (when training is complete the dog should always be 'tuned in' to its handler). It needs to be remembered that dogs have very keen hearing and if ten people all recall their dogs with the same recall but with a twenty-second interval between each owner's call, the dogs will all identify their own command! It all comes down to obedience.

Always try to tell a puppy what it is doing. For example, when it comes running to you give the 'recall' command, when it sits down give it the 'sit' command. Word association is an important part of training. Dogs do not understand English as we know it, but I taught one of my fastest little dogs, Megan, to go a pace slower to the word 'slow'. Each time Megan was running at top speed, a gallop, I would check her with a whistle and when she slowed a pace to a canter I told her 'slow'. This worked well until I forgot to think dog and became human again – when she was walking too fast I told her to go slow, and she immediately began to canter. I imagine she had a grin on her face as well! This tells us all we need to know about word association. The dog will associate the sound you make to a particular action and vice versa. You can use this method to teach the basic commands as part of everyday living. When you feed your puppy put it in the sit position and tell it 'sit', put the dish down and keep your puppy still for a moment with the 'wait' command, choose your own 'break' command and use it to give your puppy permission to eat. A 'break' command is essential, as it informs the puppy that you are giving it permission to move, play or go ahead, or that it is the end of training. As you become more at ease with training you will begin to develop your own style and form of communication, one for just

Introduce your puppy to word association and the feel of a light collar and lead as soon as possible. A puppy will soon associate the sound 'down' to the action.

you and your dog. If you relax and 'think dog', your instinct will guide your communication.

As soon as possible, get your puppy used to a light collar and lead. To begin with, just let it get used to the feel of the collar and when you attach the lead make sure you do not get into a tug of war situation, as all you will achieve is a frightened puppy. Don't allow the puppy to chew the lead – one of the first words you should teach is 'No', and now is a good time to use it. You will find in the early stages that your puppy will follow you around the house, and you can use this time to have it on a loose lead occasionally, applying gentle pressure and always being reassuring with your voice. However, don't make the mistake of 'baby talking' to your puppy; far from reassuring it all is well, for different reasons both the dominant and the nervous puppy will see it as a weakness. Your puppy needs to hear a firm but gentle voice, one that makes it feel that you are reliable and it can trust you.

The Great Outdoors

All dogs need an area where they can 'free exercise', somewhere that they can let off a little steam and play far more boisterous games than are acceptable indoors. If you allow your pup the run of the garden you could be storing up trouble for the future. A dog that has the run of the garden will soon believe it owns it, and with this ownership comes the right to dig, bark at intruders and even to bark at people passing by the gate. If you provide a run or play area for your pup and use the same 'invitation' method as you have used for your 'kennel', you will be eliminating the risk of ownership. Once again it is simple – you take your pup into the pen and let it play for a few moments, then invite it into *your* garden. A puppy or young dog brought up to know where the line of ownership lies will respect its leader. If you choose to have friends visiting, have a barbecue or have children playing in the garden your dog will be content in its own area and will not be barking or expecting to be allowed on your patch. Similarly, it has a safe area of its own should the need arise. This method will not prevent your dog from barking and letting you know if there is an intruder, but it will stop it being demanding or bad-mannered.

You cannot shield your dog from the outside world, nor should you want to. You need to be cautious until your puppy has had all its vaccinations, but if you are over-cautious you will create a nervous dog. The first three months of a dog's life are the ones that will leave an impression on it for life. Any puppy that is encouraged to be shy or lacking in confidence in these formative weeks will remain so. In the pack, 'Mum' will only allow her brood to 'cling' to her for a short while; when she feels it is time for them to stand on their own four feet she prepares them for it. There will be times when something scares her puppy and she will comfort it, but there will be other times when it runs to her from a situation it *could* have dealt with and she will push it away. We don't need to push our puppies away, just give them the confidence they need to face the world. We don't want them making their own decisions and causing fights, nor annoying

Border Collies are intelligent and the working instinct should work for you and not against you. Betty Duggan's Jem is a sheepdog and never stops working but she is educated to keep the hens in order and not to interfere with them.

Maureen Merone's Gemma is competent at competition obedience, shepherding and sheepdog trials but she is educated not to work these little charges.

other people and dogs, but neither do we want them to be frightened of them. A puppy needs to know that there is nothing for it to be frightened of because as part of your pack you will deal with any threatening situation which may arise. In other words, it has confidence and trust in its handler. When you take your puppy out you don't need to hand it over to everyone you meet in order to socialize it. However, you do need to get it used to everyday occurrences and noises such as washing machines, vacuum cleaners, cars and any other 'would-be monsters' that may loom up in or around your home.

Don't underestimate the 'power of the voice'. Just as dogs use body language to communicate with each other, so does a mother whimper and croon to her young. Your puppy needs to understand the word 'No', but in contrast it also needs to know what 'good dog' means. If you are going to let your pup know when it is breaking the rules, so must you let it know when it pleases you. If you watch a litter of puppies playing, you will notice

that one look from their mother can bring an instant stop to their game and one little snuffle of praise will produce much tail wagging and pleasure. What 'Mum' doesn't do is feed them every time they please her! I am against titbit training both with a puppy and with the older dog. Your puppy should *want* to please you, it should be pleasing you out of respect and loyalty not because it expects to receive a food reward. I am not against titbits as such, I am against titbit *training* and there is a big difference. Let's compare with children again. A parent doesn't, or shouldn't, bribe their child to clear the table, wash the pots, tidy their room, or go to bed early, with a bar of chocolate for each chore done. Nor should a reward be given when all the chores are done, for the child is being educated to be responsible and to do things which are necessary (basic obedience in the dog) at the first time of asking. Later when the child goes to school it will be given a list of tasks to do (advanced obedience) and reward will not even be feasible. When the child is an adult and goes to work it will receive a salary, or payment, not a titbit. However, the young child may, when least expecting it, receive a treat. At school a good report or a concession will be a reward. At work a job well done for a thoughtful employer may receive a bonus. All treats are worth working for. The puppy should quite happily do things to please its pack leader and will be delighted when the leader gives it praise – an unexpected treat is a bonus but should not be bribery!

A Border Collie is cunning and quick to learn. If it sees a weakness in its leader it will use it to its own advantage, and bribery is a weakness. Why else would a pack leader resort to such methods other than the fact that they feel they cannot gain the respect of their pack any other way. So what better way for a clever little collie to keep its not very determined leader on its toes than to refuse to do anything without the promise of food. I also feel bribery to be an unkind method of tuition; if a puppy is asked to sit for a titbit but doesn't do it to the human's expectations, it won't receive the titbit until it does it again and maybe even for a third time. How is that puppy to know it wasn't correct the first time and how is it to respect someone who promises and fails to deliver?

It is essential to think dog and by now you should be beginning to share a rapport with your puppy and your natural instinct should be starting to guide you. If you have put each foundation brick in its correct place you should now be able to build upwards, but there is one thing that could bring your training crashing down around you. Food!

A good friend of mine once used a term when describing my dogs, saying, they were 'giggly' collies and I thought this was a lovely description of a mischievous Border Collie. Well, some Border Collies can 'giggle' their way through life and some just shout and scream no matter how much training they get. The majority of the 'loud brigade' are living on a diet which is making them feel so high it is a wonder they are not flying! So, it's time to visit the larder!

Training Your Puppy

Don't introduce games that can develop instincts that you will not need. Your puppy does not need a myriad of toys, it needs quality time with you. Exercise of the body is necessary but it should be in addition to exercising the mind. Learn to understand your puppy's body language and lay the foundation for basic training.

Your puppy can go out with you, it can mix and socialize if a degree of common sense is used, but only if you have spent enough quality time with it for it to know who its pack leader is and where its boundaries are. The more time you spend understanding your puppy the sooner it will become well balanced and confident enough to face the world.

CHAPTER 5

Nutrition – Food for Thought!

Feeding, just like training, comes down to common sense. There was a time when food was uncomplicated and easy to understand; however, there seems to be a trend in the modern dog world to make everything as complicated, difficult to understand and expensive as possible. So let's take a look at the choices and through a process of elimination we will make the food store look less like Santa's Grotto as we find food suitable for an energetic Border Collie.

We need to go back in time again to take a good look at the ancestral collie, the pack dog. Predators are hunters and nature looks after her own, providing animals with an instinct to know what type of food they need to eat, when to eat it and where to find it. When we domesticate a wild animal we deprive it of the ability to fend for itself, and so any animal we take into our lives or homes becomes dependent on us for its well-being, including living quarters, hygiene and food. If we are to provide a diet for the well-being of the dog we need to look at its requirements; otherwise human choice may prevail and food will be selected for appearance and advertisers' statements rather than for the dog's benefit.

Just like a pride of lions, a pack of dogs will hunt, kill and devour its prey. A rest period follows where exercise and daily routine are put on hold and, because eating entails a 'lowering of the guard', the surrounding area will dictate some of the procedure. If the 'kill' was in an exposed area and too big to be moved then a sentry will be necessary, but if the kill can be taken to a 'safe house' guard duty will be minimal. If the meal was a 'banquet', the following day will be a rest day, including the digestive system, then normal everyday activities will resume. If meat is plentiful the pack will be abounding with energy and the effort needed to hunt will not be a problem. But if meat is not in plentiful supply there will still not be a shortage of food in the larder. Dogs are quite capable of equipping themselves with a 'vegetarian' cupboard, and will forage for natural vitamins and minerals. They will have a 'salad bar' and snack quite happily on mice, creepy crawlies and other wee tasty morsels. However, a shortage of meat means the pack will search for a better stocked area before the 'killing energy' ebbs. If they live entirely on snacks they will find it difficult to produce the short, high burst of energy needed to outwit and outrun their quarry. Dogs eat to satisfy their energy demand!

It is worth taking note how a pack may provide a meal. All the hunting members will have a part to play, some will stalk, some hypnotize, some outrun, some chase and some kill. All these instincts are in each member but some will be more skilful in certain areas than others. If we liken this to a tribe of Indians, each will have its own role to play within the hunting party, but although they may all excel in different areas they are still capable of performing all the different functions. All the instincts which make the Border Collie the herding dog of today are in each dog and each will have a job it would have excelled at in the wild. The prominent instinct must be recognized and the weaker one detected to enable the handler to subdue or enhance as required. But all the familiar characteristics stem from the pack survival instinct.

The feeding habits and requirements of the dog in the wild give us the clues we need to feed the domestic dog on a sensible diet. A dog does not *have* to eat meat, it can and does eat vegetation, it grazes but does not eat corn, it does rest its digestive system and it does know how and where to find certain nutrients.

Border Collies still have strong pack instincts but foraging for food, hunting, killing and devouring creepy crawlies are not acceptable in the human 'pack', so *we* must accept the responsibility for correct diet and nutrition. Feeding is personal and individual; each household will have its own ideas and not all dogs will have the same requirements. Nutritional information can be technical and confusing, leaving anyone studying the information provided on a bag or tin of dog food not only no wiser but probably more confused!

Stamina and endurance coupled with suppleness and the ability to work things out are part of the sheepdog's heritage. This dog is travelling at speed, looking where he is going and concentrating on his job at the same time while he is barely touching the ground. Too low or too high a level of nutrition will prevent a dog from being able to produce optimum performance.

Understanding Food

After many years of feeding and 'trial and error' foods, thousands of questions and hours of listening to nutritionists I have developed some very strong opinions regarding the Border Collie's nutritional requirements. I can honestly say that eighty per cent of problem cases I have dealt with in the domestic collie have been exacerbated by incorrect diet. This is through no fault of the owners, who have been trying to provide the best for their dogs, but of the information, or rather lack of it, available explaining the importance of understanding foods by learning to 'read' the packaging. Parents are usually very aware of the nutritional intake of their children's diet, taking note of information about E numbers, colourants and other additives, yet they often fail to apply a similar awareness to their dog's diet!

Border Collies are not a 'new invention' – they have been with us for a long time and they have worked, and worked hard, on the diets provided for them in the past. Whether the average diet of yesterday was sufficient or one we would select today is irrelevant, it is what this breed has adapted to. If you have a breed sheet for your collie and you look at some of the ancestors you may be pleased to see some champions in the background. But you could be surprised if you were to find out that those champions were probably fed on a diet containing a lot less energy than you may be feeding your dog.

A dog working sheep may be required to work long hours in poor weather and

It is essential to maintain a natural development for the young Border Collie, as joints and muscles will suffer if the diet is incorrect. Young Tess is running at speed, the nearside legs are off the ground and all the weight of the dog is on her offside legs which are coupled under her. Over-development would reduce the dog's suppleness and under-development would result in strain.

on rough ground. If this dog rushes out and burns up all its energy in the first few mad moments it will have nothing left to give. Stamina and endurance are needed; the dog must be able to pace itself, it must be able to think and work things out (impossible if it is working too fast), and it must be able to produce the same ability at the end of the day as it began it with. The companion collie is not required to 'work'. It may be employed in an energetic sport and it may enjoy long and varied exercise, but it is not actually 'working'. The physical exertion required to complete a day's shepherding plus the mental 'work' might not be equalled in any other form of employment. Sniffer dogs, those working with search and rescue, and dogs employed in any of the services will be 'working' and using energy. The companion collie in comparison will be using far less energy and physical effort than any of these dogs and will probably not be using its brainpower to capacity, yet its energy intake in many cases by far exceeds its requirements.

As we have already discovered through the information that the stud books and the archives have for us, the Border Collie has changed little during the last century but the diet during that time would be far different to today's diet. There would be no puppy and junior foods and food for high performance, food for resting, food for veterans and all the other choices on offer today. Most of the dogs would be fed a substantial home mix with the nutrition balanced to suit the individual. Although today's variety of dog foods makes life much simpler, with no mixing and no guess work, it is not always easy to suit the individual or even a specific breed. For example, a food manufactured for 'the working dog' may

sound simple, but for what degree of work is it catering? A food for the adult non-working dog is a food catering for dogs in general, but a Border Collie has different requirements to many other breeds. Their energy level is naturally high and what may be ideal for many breeds may be far too high in energy for the mischievous collie!

So how will you know what to feed your dog and how can the incorrect diet affect it? First of all, you need to be able to understand the food labels and this does not require trying to understand the complexities of nutrition, vitamins, minerals, how to balance them and what is digestible and what is not. The beauty of complete foods is the fact they come ready balanced, so all you need to understand is the energy level and your own dog's needs. If you spend some time browsing the shelves in the pet shop you will soon learn to understand the labels. The protein and fat/oil content are the simplest way for the beginner to 'read' the energy level. High protein is high energy, low protein will be a lower energy diet, and the fat content (energy again) will be adapted to fall in line with the protein content. There are many other ingredients and factors which are relevant, but they all fall into line with one another so we need only deal with what is necessary to make feeding easier to understand. To make a simple comparison, the average shepherding collie can be fed on anything from twenty to twenty-seven per cent protein depending on the type of work and the physical exertion demanded. Very few will be fed on twenty-seven per cent and to justify this level there will need to be a specific reason (such as work load, temperament, and so on). So most sheepdogs will have a diet of between twenty to twenty-four per cent, whereas the average companion collie will be receiving the same level and in many cases higher, while not being asked to do any form of 'work'!

What is 'Hyper'?

A Border Collie fed on high-energy food that is not using that energy will show all the symptoms of being hyperactive. A hyperactive dog is a problem dog, because even if it is controllable the handler is always aware that the dog must be kept occupied and this constant attention to keep the dog out of mischief creates yet another set of problems. If we remove ourselves from the dog situation we can make more comparisons. Most people will have heard of the affect oats have on horses – feeding oats to a horse and then keeping it without exercise will make it harder to hold, nervous and can make it act out of character. If an adolescent human, who is not used to the effects of drink, consumes a large amount of alcohol, that adolescent will become drunk. In a state of drunkenness he or she will behave out of character and may even commit a crime, which under sober circumstances they would not have contemplated. Similarly, a Border Collie fed on high-energy food can become 'drunk'! The results can manifest themselves differently according the dog's character and temperament. It may become nervous or aggressive, too energetic, bad-mannered, difficult to handle, nippy, and it may also turn to destruction, tail chasing, bird chasing, whining and yapping. All of these problems will

A group of happy collies taking time out with their owners. The ages of these collies vary from two to twelve years old and work is from trainee to retirement. Careful feeding of the correct levels of nutrition enables them all not only to look as fit as one another but to be able to enjoy life to the full.

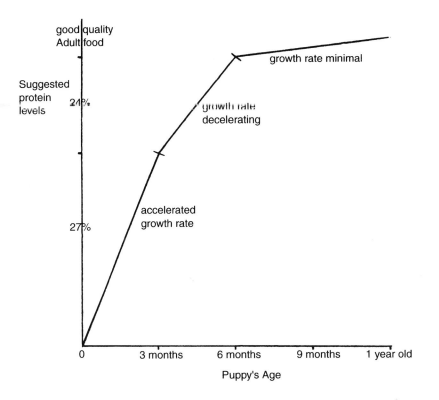

good quality
Adult food

Suggested
protein
levels

24%

growth rate minimal

growth rate
decelerating

accelerated
growth rate

27%

0   3 months   6 months   9 months   1 year old

Puppy's Age

This graph shows the puppy's age in relation to its nutritional requirements. Note the decline in growth rate from three to six months and again from six months to one year. The protein levels given are a guide but age and natural growth must govern the food intake and the dog's natural growth must be catered for, if not physical and mental problems may occur.

have arisen, to explain it simply, from the dog becoming intoxicated because the owners have unwittingly provided a 'drinks bar' to a family member who should remain teetotal!

There are always exceptions to the rule and some dogs will respond in a different manner to others. Kim, one of my collies, was always a slightly lazy 'little being', working well but never above and beyond the call of duty. More than once Kim slowed her work down to allow another dog to take on the larger share of the workload, but once fed on twenty-four per cent protein she became more willing to 'do her bit'. However, Kim's kennel mates on twenty-four per cent protein were difficult to control and almost impossible to stop!

An adult dog may be receiving an adult food of a sensible energy level but still be showing all the symptoms of the hyperactive collie. In this case, the early feeding regime will have played an important role in the dog's behaviour. A puppy will be fed on puppy food and then reduced to junior food, but many will not have been given a lower, more settling diet until they are almost one year old. The average Border Collie puppy can treble in growth up to three months old but only grow half as much again up to six months old, then will fill out and mature with another possible inch of growth (these are only approximate examples for the purpose of explaining growth foods). If puppy food is designed to see the puppy through its initial growth period it should be reduced in intensity at approximately three months old. If junior food is designed to see the dog through the next stage it should be reduced at the end of that stage. Growing food is designed to help the youngster develop, for the bones to be strong and healthy and to give energy through the period of life when the body is working on its own initiative, that is, growing. If this food is administered when the body no longer requires it the extra level of nutrition becomes surplus to requirements and is often utilized in a non-constructive manner – high energy!

Dog food is manufactured for dogs in general and it would not be cost-affective for the manufacturers to design food for each specific breed. For example, for health reasons, I know I should not consume too much wheat but most foods contain wheat. If I go to a specialist shop and buy food designed for my type of diet it is extremely expensive, but I can eat a normal diet and add and omit sensibly, according to requirements and my state of health at the time. So to feed the average Border Collie on a sensible level of nutrition the food needs to be selected and fed according to each dog's requirements. The manufacturers supply all the necessary details on the packaging – the dog owner just needs to learn to read before purchase.

When a new owner collects their puppy they should be advised on puppy food, but many problem adolescent collies will have been fed on the breeder's instructions so there are a few factors you need to be aware of. High-energy puppy food will have a litter of pups looking solid and well grown, nothing wrong with this, but if the food has done its job and the puppies have good growth maybe now

A Border Collie has the build of an athlete but few people realize the amount of strain on the legs in just normal exercise. This dog is running towards its handler, not only is its weight on one front leg but the body is travelling forwards and downwards.

would be the time to reduce a little. You don't need to change the food immediately but be aware that the level of nutrition needs to be monitored. If a lower nutritional level of puppy food is used from the start, then the puppy can be kept on it a little longer so avoiding the necessity to keep changing foods. A young puppy may be fed four times a day and the nutritional intake of these feeds must be taken into consideration. Four feeds of cereal will not be enough in nutritional value but four feeds of high or neat protein may be too much; dogs do not eat percentage protein, they eat grams per day so the daily requirement should be divided between the number of feeds and not per feed. Each person and dog has different standards and requirements and I am trying to avoid being technical or confusing; quite simply, the higher the protein and nutritional value of the food the shorter the period of time you need to feed it. I do not feel there is a need to feed a Border Collie on junior food, but it is for each individual to decide their own dog's diet. Junior food became available with the advent of many and varied dog foods; if you are feeding a sensible puppy food, your youngster is manageable, you are happy with both his growth and energy level and your preference is for junior food make sure you select a sensible type. If the puppy food is of twenty-seven per cent or less then the same brand of junior food will be balanced in accordance. Not all dog food manufacturers produce junior food; if I feed a twenty-seven per cent puppy food I simply reduce to a sensible good quality adult food of a slightly lower level, according to condition and growth, maybe a good food of twenty-four per cent. This is my guideline and I can adjust according to fitness condition. I never weigh my puppies – a watched pot never boils and the best way to monitor puppies' condition and growth rate is by 'eye and hands on'. If you are inexperienced or feel happier monitoring the weight gain, don't allow it to become an obsession.

Choosing a 'complete' food simplifies feeding and the nutritional requirements are balanced for you, so if you choose to feed a different diet beware any pitfalls the novice can fall into. Tinned meat appears to have a low protein level but the moisture content is high, and when the mixer 'energy' and the meat 'energy' are combined you may be feeding a much higher level than you think. There are many 'new' ideas on diet, such as feeding raw foods, all-meat meals and self-mixing; in fact, these concepts are not new but are the diets of the past century. For those who know exactly what they are doing (and very few dog owners are canine dieticians), know how to balance the feeds and add the correct vitamins and minerals at the right level, there is nothing wrong with self-mixing. However, to do this the owner needs to understand the feeding regime of the pack dog and be able to translate this correctly to the modern dog. Feeding raw food would seem to relate to natural feeding methods, but the dog in the wild would be eating meat still warm from the kill (fresh meat) and would eat everything required for a balanced diet. If the dog was eating a cold kill or old meat it would have available all the natural resources for keeping any gut problems at bay; the natural dog knows how to make nature its friend. Humans will find it difficult, if not impossible, to supply the dog with the same natural food found in the wild or food free from additives. There is no such

In the dark Floss's leg action is hesitant, the tail denotes the slower pace and the legs are not working diagonally as one may suppose they should. Her body weight is made 'light' whilst she stalks.

A movement in the dark calls for action and Floss moves with all her weight thrown forwards onto one leg.

thing as 'fresh' meat for a domestically fed dog. Before the meat comes to the butchers it is already an 'old kill' as far as the dog is concerned, and it is also meat from an animal that as far as nature is concerned has not been reared naturally. Wild dogs kill to eat and eat to kill; the domestic dog does not need to kill to eat so it makes sense not to supply it with killing energy in its food! Tests done in the past have proved that dogs maintained for over a year on biscuit plus raw meat supplemented with minerals and vitamins were no different in health or appearance from dogs maintained on other foods. Raw meat is more likely to cause digestive upsets and can carry the risk of infection that the dog will be unable to 'cure' through its own natural resources. In domestication we prevent the dog from having the availability of a natural diet and digestive medication, so there is little point in trying to emulate this diet unless we can guarantee it to be perfectly natural and balanced. Providing the dog with correct nutrients is paramount for its health and if there is any doubt as to the correct balance of home mixing or raw food then I would advise a good complete food with the correct energy level for your dog's health. The best of diets cannot be efficient if there is an internal parasite problem and from puppies through to adults my dogs are wormed on a very regular basis and then four times a year, once again subject to condition and habits (many dogs have unsavoury eating habits).

Natural Development

A dog eats to satisfy its energy demand and few non-working Border Collies will need the kind of energy found in high protein food. Food must be balanced; for example, a biscuit which has been manufactured for feeding with meat should not be fed on its own in order to lower the protein level as the other nutrients will have been balanced for a supplement diet and not a complete diet. If an adult dog is fed energy in excess of its requirements it can become hyperactive, and if a puppy is fed energy in excess of its growing requirements it can have growth problems. A puppy developing naturally in the pack will instinctively eat for a natural growth rate, reaching maturity at a later date than many pet collies, and it will also indulge in 'free exercise'. There will be running, twisting and turning, but no more than is natural for a litter of pups to develop. At a later stage the older dogs will teach the youngsters what might appear to be a game of 'tag',

but they are in fact preparing them for the kind of agile skills needed to catch their prey when they reach maturity. At no time will a puppy be subjected to over-indulgence or exhaustion.

If a puppy is fed on a high level of nutrition for too long a period its body can become overdeveloped; if it grows too quickly too soon stress can be inflicted on some of the joints and damage may occur. Not all cases of HD are genetic – some are Hip Damage. I have seen several cases of young Border Collies who have had HD and their histories have all been similar. As youngsters these dogs were fed on high protein diets and supplements and received excessive exercise with too much hip work (twisting, turning and jumping), resulting in weak and damaged hips. There is no race involved in the development a young dog; the criteria should be for 'natural growth', feeding a sensible level of nutrition and not over-exercising. Border Collies are not big, heavy dogs; they are bred to be nimble. The need to monitor a puppy's growth rate and to feed according to that requirement in the early stages is essential. Reducing the 'growing energy' nutrition as the growth rate slows down and allowing the final filling out of the body to be done as a natural process will give a young dog's body the chance to develop at its own speed.

Dogs do not become bored with food, therefore they do not need to keep having their diet changed and coloured food does not impress them. Confronted with a large selection of dog food to choose from it is often tempting for owners to select what appeals to them rather than working out what the dog really needs. Highly coloured food may look attractive but to the dog it is just food, so make sure the ingredients meet your dog's require-ments. Plain-looking food may appear bland and unattractive, but if the nutri-tional content is what your dog needs then that is the food for you to choose. Each brand of food will provide feeding instructions, so make sure you are feed-ing the correct amount of food for your dog's weight; the amounts given are only a guideline and you must always feed to condition. The healthy adult dog fed once a day should look for its food and lick its dish clean. If it does not eat all of its food it does not mean it is bored with the menu; providing it is healthy it may just need to rest its digestive system. If a child leaves vegetables on the plate he or she will often accept a 'sticky bun', so a dog will force its digestive system to work if you provide the equivalent of the 'sticky bun' just because it did not lick its dish clean! A dog soon works out that it can change its menu by refusing to eat the food offered and the more it uses this power the more tasty the menu has to become. If a dog is hungry it will eat, but that does not mean you must never change the diet. Just like human beings, some dogs have certain foods which may disagree with their digestive system, but when a food is acceptable and palatable then only change it for the nutritional value, for example, veteran, vegetarian or energy level. A dog in the wild will eat both meat and vegetation, not for variety but to obtain the necessary nutrients,

Dogs in their own natural environment will find the vegetation necessary for a healthy digestive system. Through domestication they no longer roam and are denied this natural access. Modern natural food is no longer natural for the dog, so adaptations must be made.

Dogs love bones and the right kind of bone is essential for their well-being. In his own area and left to his own devices Pip will chew on a bone for hours, deriving the goodness from it and maintaining healthy teeth.

and if you feed a complete food the dog's nutritional requirements will be catered for without the need for the dog to 'forage'. Dogs do graze and there are certain grasses they like to sample, but grazing is not necessarily a sign of a problem stomach; it is their way of cleaning out their system. However, not all grazing ends in a 'clean up' – quite often it is an additive.

When choosing a brand of food don't be confused by the varieties. Most have been developed for a reason; for example, vegetarian food can be beneficial for allergies and the protein is not as high in energy as meat protein. Chicken and rice, and lamb and rice are good foods for dogs with gastric problems and once again the energy is slightly less than the red meat energy. There is no need for a Border Collie to be overweight, for there are special weight-reducing diets available, but always make sure you feed for the weight your dog should be and not to its excess weight level. Gluten-free foods are among many of the special diets available and are beneficial for problems such as stiff joints and arthritis.

It is natural for dogs to graze. Tip does not have a problem and is not poorly. He is enjoying reverting to the call of the natural dog, selecting herbage which he can utilize and grass which will clean his gut.

Food is an important part of your dog's life, but there is no need for it ever to become a problem. Know your dog's temperament and its natural energy level and then feed accordingly. When you discover the food that makes both you and your dog happy don't be tempted to change it unless you believe it to be for the best. I know of two dog owners who changed their dogs' diets, on the recommendation of 'someone who was in authority', and within two months their well-behaved and obedient collies had turned into barking, nipping hooligans. It took twice as long to 'sober them up' and as long again to retrain them!

Remember: choose your food with care to keep your dog fit and healthy with a natural energy level, and keep him sober!

Feeding Your Collie Correctly

Feed your dog to its growth and energy requirements. Don't feed an energetic Border Collie on a high-energy diet; the average non-working collie is often fed incorrectly on a higher energy level than a working collie! It is not complicated learning the basics of feeding requirements, and the little effort needed is worth it for your dog's health and behaviour. Don't feel guilty that your dog may not be eating as it would in the wild, it is impossible to feed a domestic dog as 'naturally' as if it were in a pack.

Healthy adult dogs need only be fed once a day. In the wild they kill, eat to capacity and then rest their gut for a day, after which they can either kill again or graze. We may fill the domestic dog but we do not rest their gut for a day, so if we are feeding a meal each day we must allow a substantial rest period between feeds. A domestic dog should not be fed 'ad-lib' as it will not fill its gut and then rest it, or nibble as if it were grazing.

CHAPTER 6

Creating a Partnership

When you introduce a puppy or a dog into your home, you are not only mixing two different packs but two different species! You have to learn to integrate, to understand each other and to become one pack, and you must also establish who is to be pack leader. If a human being leaves their country of origin and re-establishes in another country, he or she will endeavour to learn as much as possible about the different culture and language in order to make it easier to integrate. Dogs do not enter our homes and lives of their own choosing; they have their own 'culture', their instincts are strong and they have their own rules and code of ethics. We introduce them into our lives because we want them to be there, so *we* must endeavour to understand *them*. If we undertake the task of learning about their instincts, their pack rules and their language, we will be better equipped to explain to them about our way of life and our rules, and we will also be able to communicate as a pack leader and not as a pack member.

Dogs do not feel the cold as we humans do. Either shepherding or out walking human beings need protection against the elements but these two dogs with their sleek winter coats and natural vitality will not feel the cold as their owner will.

One of the magical qualities of a Border Collie is its ability to be able to work both with you and for you. They will do what they are asked to do whilst working for you but are more than willing to work with you, giving above and beyond the call of duty out of loyalty and respect. So what is the difference? A shepherd who is in control of his dog will give commands for it to follow; he is in charge as the pack leader. But, for a shepherd who has formed a bond with his dog, the same dog will give his all on a dark, cold night without a word being spoken. Cold, wet and tired they may be, but dog and man will work together until the job is done. The man is still the pack leader! A collie will give its best no matter what its profession, but it will always be able to produce something 'extra' for the person who is able to combine being a pack leader with being a partner.

The first few days with your puppy are the most important, for in that time you will either become pack leader, or your position will become negotiable. If you introduce an older dog into your home you may find that negotiation does not come into the equation! A puppy is in new surroundings and for the first few days is dependent on you for security; if you provide it with a secure 'home' of its own and use the 'wait to enter my house' rule you will already be establishing hierarchy. There should never be a need to chastise your puppy for not conforming to pack law as it should be anxious to please you – all you need to do is explain correctly. There is a difference between a puppy being 'out of order' or just exercising its humour and its inquisitive right to touch the perimeters of your boundaries. Above all, when dealing with a Border Collie you must retain your sense

of humour and recognize naughty from mischievous! It takes time to build a relationship, it comes with trust and respect and these cannot be gained without the dog feeling it has a leader it can rely on. The foundation for this bonding begins in the first few weeks.

There is a saying regarding human beings that the first seven years of life influence their future. The first few weeks of a puppy's life can affect its reactions to many everyday occurrences that we might not even notice, and if we do notice them we may not handle them correctly! I have lost track of the number of times a worried owner has brought a 'problem' collie to me, concerned at the dog's reactions to motorbikes or the vacuum cleaner, washer, spray can, and so on. There are usually two main reasons for the dog's behaviour – one is that it is born out of fear, and two is that the owner has, inadvertently, encouraged that fear.

Noise Sensitivity

A puppy born in a house may be used to sounds of the washing machine and vacuum cleaner and it will have had the security of its mother from which to draw strength and acceptance, but it may not be used to many of the outdoor sounds.

On the other hand, a puppy born outside or on a farm will be used to many of the outdoor sounds but may be horrified the first time it hears the washing machine. The words 'security of its mother from which to draw strength' tell us the puppy needs to feel safe, and with this safety comes confidence. When it enters your home it has lost its security, you provide it a 'safe house' in the form of its own den, and now you must become the 'rock' upon which it can rely. But a good leader does not make a dog so dependent that it cannot think for itself; the dog still has to live within the pack community and must be able to work things out for itself. There is a fine balance between being the leader and having a confident, trusting dog (pack), or of being totally in control and taking away the dog's ability to work things out for itself. A collie is intelligent and has a marvellous memory; these are attributes the pack leader can use to advantage in training and the dog will love 'giving' these qualities to a leader it respects. Only if you fail to establish yourself as pack leader will the dog's ability to work things out go against you, and you will find he is busy organizing a 'role reversal'!

During the first few days in its new environment the puppy does not need the added stress of new noises, so these could be 'put on hold' or made when he is feeling confident. For example, if his bed were next to the washing machine it would be unfair to put the machine on when he is asleep and feeling safe. He needs to be able to come to terms with the noise when he is feeling confident and you are able to alleviate any concerns he may have. It is how you handle these concerns which can affect the rest of the puppy's life.

A dog that was brought to me terrified of motorbikes had never had any reason to be afraid of one, according to the owner, but how good a memory has the owner? If a motorbike roared past when the puppy was in its formative months it may have been terrified and the owner not have noticed the degree of fear. The puppy could have been held close and given sympathy, cuddles and protection, it may even have caused a chuckle among the family as it ran scurrying back to them. But if the fear was not noticed the puppy will have drawn its own conclusions about the monster bike. If the puppy was given fuss and sympathy the owner will probably have convinced it the bike *was* a monster, and if its flight of fear caused amusement (and this is easily done without realizing) the puppy will not feel safe within its pack. The same responses can apply to almost any noise that takes the puppy by surprise and may be responsible for a dog having problems when it matures.

Relate back to children – if thunder frightens a child and the parents try to make the child feel secure by hiding under the table with it, the child immediately feels that thunder is to hide from. If the parents do not encourage hiding but provide hugs and cuddles and tell the child they will protect it from the thunder the child still believes thunder is frightening. If the parents give hugs and cuddles, enough to calm the youngster, and then proceed as normal whilst providing a simple explanation for thunder, the child will still feel safe and protected with the parents but will also know, on this occasion, that there is nothing to fear.

The same method applies to a puppy. If fear makes it run to its bed go to it, stroke it and if you sense it is reluctant to come out of the bed and face the 'monster' carry on about your business, talking calmly to it all the time. Your body language will be telling the puppy there is nothing to fear for *you* are not in the least bit concerned and your voice, although gentle, is strong and reassuring. If you resort to the equivalent of hiding

A puppy is naturally inquisitive and can rarely resist getting into mischief.

Try to make sure you are around to help him if he gets into difficulties – this little chap could end up 'tipping the bucket'.

under the table or being over-protective the puppy will not associate you with security – how can it if you appear to be as frightened as it is? But if you resist the urge to over-protect the puppy, it will soon begin to look to you for guidance. This is the beginning of a trusting relationship.

Border Collies have keen hearing and a noise that may not cause concern for human beings can often be stressful for them. High-pitched noises and loud bangs are the commonest 'problem' noises and although some dogs are naturally noise sensitive they are in the minority. The first fourteen weeks of a puppy's life are the formative weeks for familiarization and socialization, but the hearing has not adjusted at this early age to the many everyday noises we take for granted. Encourage your puppy to be an individual by allowing it the opportunity to be inquisitive in safe circumstances, but if it is about to investigate something that may cause it to become alarmed try to divert its attention to something more confidence-giving. For example, a puppy about to approach a cat could be frightened by the reception it receives, but a puppy examining a harmless object is using its inquisitive nature to find out about the world. The vacuum cleaner is not quite such a monster when it is quiet, and close investigation could even earn praise and encouragement from the pack leader. Examining the wonders of the new world together will not only be the beginning of forging a partnership but it will help the puppy settle in its new environment. There are only two places in a pack, leader or member, so if human and dog form a partnership and the former is the protective partner, then he or she will become the stronger, more dominant one and will be recognized as pack leader.

Just as the first few weeks are an important time for a puppy to become accustomed to its new life it is also a time of great sensitivity, and if it is chastized in a way that causes fear or alarm it can become nervous and introvert. Think back a moment to toilet training and the puppy who sees no wrong in choosing its 'own spot'; it is an easy mistake to make a sudden rush and swoop the puppy up and out of the door. The poor little chap will have no idea what it did wrong but will know to be very wary of this human in future. At this sensitive, vulnerable age, a puppy can easily be made permanently 'hand shy'. Unfortunately, the owner may not even realize what has happened and will probably think the puppy is just of the nervous type!

Word Association

As you spend time with a new puppy, you should be striving to build up a relationship and to teach basic good manners. Your puppy does not understand your language so you should try to teach it by word association, for example each time it runs to you give it the recall command. This does not have to be a specific word, but it does need to be something you are comfortable with and ensure that you make it a 'happy' and inviting sound. It does not need to be a shrill pitch and neither need it be loud. Your puppy needs to be educated to listen for your voice, so try to train quietly and use your own tone with just a slightly different pitch. Your 'wavelength' will never become familiar to your dog if you are constantly offering 'high' sounds. If you use this recall every time your puppy comes to you it will soon associate sound with action. The mistake many make is to keep calling when the puppy diverts its attention in the hope it will eventually 'switch back on'. If you do not get a response, go straight to the wee chap and gently bring him back to base, sit him down where you recalled and make sure you have his attention, tell him what a clever little being he is and let him continue with his business. Far better to explain now when only a few yards separate you than to wait until he is a little bigger, a little more cheeky and a lot further away!

Word association is one of the easiest and simplest methods of tuition – simply tell your dog what it is doing and it will soon link sound to action. The breakdown

The author is spending time getting Pip used to her 'wavelength' and redirecting his focus onto her next action.

Pip is now focused on the author's intentions and has his right ear flicked back waiting for the next sounds.

in tuition comes through transmitting the incorrect sound for the dog to associate with a certain action. For example, telling a dog to sit twice or three times transmits as 'sit multiplied by three equals the action'. From the dog's point of view why not, it allows more freedom? Recalling your pup whilst it is running the opposite way and it has not yet learned the sound will tell it that recall means keep on running. Using 'stay' when a creeping action is in progress explains 'stay' means 'creep'. Common sense tells us that it is wrong to chastise a dog for something it did several hours earlier, it needs to associate voice and action, but then we fail to be consistent when the actions are for good manners and basic training.

Teaching good manners should be an ongoing process – parents don't make a decision one day that they will teach their children how to behave in company the next day, and how to say thank you the next, it is a continuing process. If you wait until your puppy has lived with you for several weeks before you begin to teach manners he will already have established his own rules. And why not, if in those first few weeks his actions, which may have been bad-mannered, have met with no explanation of any other way of behaving? It is not fair on the youngster suddenly to begin to change his own established routine for the one you should have introduced in the very beginning!

Socialization

Socialization is a fashionable word to use. Dogs have been part of our lives for far longer than many of the modern training methods and they have not all been shy, introvert and nervous, and neither did they attend special classes designed for socializing or have their own personal psychologist! It is we who like to socialize. There are far more opportunities now for dog owners than there used to be and many different kinds of competitions. It is natural for people to want to be able to take their dogs into public places without fear of being either shown up or of losing control. A puppy needs to be socialized but this does not mean it will be nervous if it is not taken out to meet everything and everybody; in fact some puppies can suffer from too much exposure. Remember the introvert and extrovert puppies? A shy puppy taken out and made to meet everyone at the local dog club and family and friends before it has learned who is pack leader and who it can trust can soon become frightened and nervous. So will the shy puppy suffer if it is kept inside, protected from the world and every slight noise? The extrovert puppy taken out and about before it has established good manners can become unruly and arrogant, but if kept inside and over-protected it can also become nervous.

Nervousness can manifest itself in more ways than one; a nervous puppy can be shy but if forced into a leadership position, when this would not normally be its natural position, it may turn to nervous aggression. If the handler fails to become a convincing leader the nervous puppy or young dog will not be able to trust him or her and will be forced to assume leadership if, for example, a strange dog or person approaches. There are two courses of action for the youngster – run or hope a show of aggression will persuade the offending newcomer to change direction.

Once the human being is established as a reliable pack leader who can be trusted, the dog (pack) will integrate and attend family functions, dog clubs and competitions without a moment's hesitation. What is more, it will want to be attentive to its leader, to listen and to please; in fact you will have become a partnership.

Puppy Classes

Should you take your puppy to puppy socialization classes? Before you make any decisions visit the class without your pup and see what the format is. Puppy classes are designed to socialize puppies, but socialize them with what? If two packs of dogs or two tribes of Indians meet they do not all run around together like hooligans and integrate with each other. The adults will mix, and at the Big Chief's discretion so will the mature youngsters, and the remainder will only be allowed to integrate when their leader is confident he can command their attention at the first time of asking. Can you do this with your pup when it is mixing with ten or fifteen other puppies? Does it know without a shadow of a doubt that you are its pack leader or may it be forgiven for thinking that all those other pups (its own kind after all) are a pack and that it is to become part of them? Think very carefully about how and when you socialize your puppy. Many clubs have a sensible attitude to training and pack leadership, but some are following fashion without understanding the basic requirements of a dog in training. Always visit first and join in later. If you do not like what you see you are under no obligation, but if you are satisfied with the methods a good trainer will be happy to

talk to you about your own thoughts on training your dog. Puppy classes are not mandatory and they are not always in the best interest of puppies and handlers. If puppy classes worked and taught handlers how to control, socialize and train (training being ongoing), then there would be no need for the 'pre-beginners' and 'beginners' classes that are on offer at the same clubs!

Chasing

Chasing is a mindless exercise and one a puppy would not do in the wild without purpose. A litter of puppies will be taught by their elders the game of hunt and catch. Chasing very rarely culminates in the prey being caught, so early education is to dissuade the youngsters from venturing after a prey they will be unable to catch. Similarly, if a shepherd allows a young dog to approach a flock of fast-moving sheep and it is unable to travel fast enough to run around them it will follow and chase. This will make the dog excitable and will result in it using its teeth if it catches them and being both dispirited and annoyed if it doesn't. Constant ball throwing until the dog becomes overexcited is simulating chase. Running after children or adults in a game is simulating chase. Tuggy games, running with other youngsters and mouthing each other, nipping at the vacuum cleaner or bicycle wheels, all seem harmless but all are arousing an instinct you may wish you had left dormant! Never let your puppy become excited to the point of being hysterical, think about its every action and game, for what seems good fun at four months old can be an absolute menace at fourteen months old.

Note the body language of the dog in the diagram; tail erect, body stiff and pulling back on the haunches. Playing with a litter-mate this language would be accompanied by growling and 'playful' aggression. A game of 'tuggy' may seem harmless but in many cases it not only overexcites a young dog it encourages it to use its teeth. Not only can this result in the dog being destructive it can also cause a problem where young children and toys are concerned.

Where to Live and When to Feed

You will come across so many rules on feeding and where your dog should and should not go in your house, that if you pay attention to them all you will have your house full of baby gates and time clocks! This is your dog and it goes where you want and it eats when you decide to feed it; the golden rule is *you* make the decisions and not your dog! Feeding has proven to be a controversial subject for many trainers and handlers and the different ideas and regimes are often very confusing. How many feeds a day each dog has should not be down to human choice or preference, but when to feed a dog can be. A puppy will need four feeds a day at first, but from three months onwards this should be reduced to three feeds and, according to health and condition, reduced to two feeds between four and six months. Many dog owners find it

hard to resist the temptation of too much, too often and the result is overfeeding. A healthy adult dog does not require more than one feed a day and this can be offered at a time to suit you, your circumstances and your dog's habits. Dogs have a twenty-four-hour digestive system, which means that the feeds need to be at approximately the same time each day. If you feed at exactly the same time the dog will soon become a creature of habit and although consistency makes for good education and training, habit can become demanding. If your dog's system calls for a visit to the designated toilet three hours after feeding it would be unwise to feed it late at night; once again you need to know your dog and be confident in making your own decisions.

In my opinion, there is absolutely no need to follow the rule of 'your dog must not be fed until after you have eaten' in order to prove leadership. The day that man joins his dog in hunting, killing and

A well-educated dog will 'wait' for his food when asked to do so but it is unfair to keep taking it away from him for if he has been taught the acceptable mental and physical boundaries he will respect your rules. It is far better to teach him manners and to provide him with his own area than to use his food for conformation of his manners. If you are in control and he is part of your pack you should not need such conformation.

eating the prey together on the ground, or the dog sits with 'bib and tucker' at the table brandishing a knife and fork there is no common eating ground to prove or disprove leadership. This does not mean that the dog should be begging at the table or receiving titbits, as this is encouraging bad manners and bad habits. Nor is it a good idea to feed your dog at the same time as your family meal unless it is in a separate area. If a dog knows it is going to be fed either at the same time as its owner or just afterwards it will begin looking for food when the human meal is being prepared, an excellent argument for not feeding it after your meal! Dogs live by pack rule and human beings often interpret pack law in human terms and this does not work; we have to see it from the dogs mind. They wait until the pack leader has taken his fill of the prey they caught as a pack, but the food they salvage and take for the family or the food they forage is eaten when the pack leader does not require their services. They will, however, be aware that they have a leader who can,if he wishes, sample their food but usually

only when he thinks he may be dealing with an insubordinate. He is usually confident enough not to have to keep displaying authority, as these kind of unnecessary bully tactics would cause unrest within the pack. Pack law has now just explained that you can feed your dog whenever you wish but it is unfair to keep 'testing' your dog by taking his food from him, something many trainers advise handlers to do.

The theory behind making sure you can take your dog's food from him whenever you wish is to enforce your position as pack leader and to ensure the dog will not cause a problem should a child try to remove the dish. The pack leader does not use food for authority, he *is* authority, and the event of children removing the dish should not arise if the dog is fed in its 'safe' area and the child is brought up to respect the dog. If your dog respects you there will never be a problem if you need to remove his food, and if he has been educated correctly he will 'wait' for your permission to eat and then he should be free to eat. For my part, if I was eating a well looked forward to meal and some idiot kept taking it away I would probably feel like strangling him! However, if he explained, in a language I could understand, that on this particular occasion it was necessary, then I would not have a problem with it. See it from the dog's point of view – his food is there for him to eat but if you need it you will take it, he knows that, so why keep taking it if you don't intend to keep it?

The issue of where your dog should be allowed to go in your house is far simpler, anywhere *you* want it to go, but with your permission. I have had many distraught owners tearfully explaining that they have always fed their dog after them, it has not been allowed upstairs and is confined to the kitchen or utility room during the day, so why is it such a menace? Because it owns the house and is entitled to do as it pleases!

Cage training, if done correctly, explains in the first few hours who owns what, and when this is established the cage door is kept open or the bed or blanket inside it can be moved to other quarters and the dog will still own only its bed. If not, you become in danger of owning a very expensive dog kennel! It does not affect your dog's behaviour if you refuse it permission to go upstairs; it simply means it hasn't been upstairs to claim it. The theory is that the dog should not be higher than the pack leader, but I have seen many bad-mannered dogs that have never been upstairs and many dogs that appear to have the run of the house with impeccable manners.

There is a difference between a dog having the run of the house and *appearing* to have the run of the house. A dog with manners and respect will be able to

Meg is used to having a rug in her bed so if she is going on a visit or is staying overnight anywhere she is quite content to sit anywhere on her 'mobile' rug.

Maureen Merone has always taught Gemma to wait at doors and gates. It is now a natural procedure for Gemma to follow and Maureen can continue on a pleasurable walk without having the problem of her dog pushing ahead and maybe getting into trouble.

enter any room, go upstairs and have apparent freedom of the house but this freedom will be with the owner's permission and will not be without certain rules. A bad-mannered dog without respect will assume ownership of any room in which it is allowed freedom. Your puppy needs to have both mental and physical boundaries. It must know where it can go and must learn when it is necessary to seek permission to do so. It must also learn when it may be acceptable to take things for granted and that this privilege must be earned!

If you are gaining your puppy's love and respect it will want to follow you wherever you go; after all, you are its new pack leader and its security, but pack leaders demand privacy. The devotion of the mother it has just left behind had its boundaries and there would be times when she would have chastised her brood for following her, enforcing some of her own boundary rules. It is a wonderful

feeling when this little four-legged friend follows you in and out of the garden and around the house. But this is also a little four-legged 'think machine' and in no time at all you will find it barging along in front of you with absolutely no regard for you or your feelings. If your youngster follows you from kitchen to sitting room make it sit and wait a moment and then invite it to follow you. If it shows no wish to follow you, preferring to play with a ball or chew a bone, call it to you and make it aware that you require its attention before it can continue with its own pursuits. Compare the education of a young dog to the education of a five-year old child. For example, it is not acceptable for children to push in front of adults when going through doors, nor to change channels on television, stay out late or interrupt conversations without first seeking permission. Each family has its own rules of acceptability and these must be adhered to by youngsters until such time that the boundaries are well estab-lished and liberties may be taken without any breakdown in authority. It is not necessary or practical to make a puppy stand and wait each time it goes through a door or wishes to follow you, but it is necessary to make sure that bad manners are not being displayed and that rules are not being ignored.

Your dog should want to follow you and be with you, but it should not presume it can do so. It must get used to the idea that permission may not always be granted. It is not difficult to insist that a dog stays behind and does not follow you when you have no choice, for example when going to work or shopping. It is difficult to remember to make a dog wait for a few seconds before going in the garden, out for a walk or just entering another room, as this is optional and therefore not always adhered to. A dog asked to wait for a few seconds before being given permission by hierarchy to enter the living room will know the living room belongs to hierarchy. A dog who lives in the kitchen should have its own 'kennel' (bed, basket, blanket, and so on) and should occasionally be made to sit there quietly while hierarchy makes a meal, reads a paper or has a drink. The dog can have a bone or a ball and can amuse itself in its own home but must remain there until given permission to re-enter hierarchy's home. This simple, short exercise will ensure that the dog does not take over the kitchen. Again, compare this with child-rearing. It should not be necessary to harass children con-stantly with rules – they should be taught, occasionally refreshed and finally each child should become a family mem-ber with its own individuality within the family circle. If you apply this to a puppy it will not take long for it to realize that your home is to be respected and that good manners reap their own reward. A dog who is well-mannered and respects its pack leader soon becomes able to have privileges. It will no longer be necessary to wait to enter a room, and it will know when it is able to visit the best room and when it must give way to visitors. This is all part of becoming a partnership and understanding each other's require-ments; it is the Indian chief to his tribe, the pack leader to his pack and parent to his child. They all live in harmony, respect each other and the tribe/pack/children are all freethinking individuals with good manners.

The rules in your home must be your own, but they must be sensible. For example, it is not fair to allow the puppy to sit on the furniture when you have no intention of allowing the same freedom when it has muddy paws. Placing a cover on the furniture makes little difference to a young dog; chairs are chairs whether they are covered are not. If you prefer your dog to be restricted to downstairs make sure everyone in the house under-stands the rule, as a dog cannot be blamed for sitting at the top of the stairs if one member of the family allows it this access occasionally. If you are happy for your dog to sit on the furniture or to have access to upstairs you have to make sure your dog understands these are privi-leges and that you are the sole owner of the property and its contents. Don't allow it to presume it can get on *your* furniture or go up *your* stairs whenever it feels like it. Children will have access to certain household items and not to others, but they will also know that these items are not theirs to own, and that they often have to ask permission for this use!

Make Your Own Rules

You have to decide what you think is going to be acceptable for yourself, your family and your dog. It may be that you do not expect a dog trainer and one who specializes in Border Collies (a breed I describe as being manipulative) to write in a book that your dog can sit on the furniture, go upstairs and be fed before you have eaten! I do not try to make the rules for dog owners, I try to help them to understand their dogs, and I would be a poor trainer if I recommended that everyone kept their dogs in the kitchen when mine have the run of the house. I believe there is far too much emphasis put on rules and regulations in the modern dog world and this makes life complicated for the dog owners who are trying to do their best but are suddenly so bogged down with such a long list of dos and don'ts that they don't have time to train for reading!

I am not recommending you allow your dog to jump all over the furniture, but you have taken it into your family and you want to enjoy it, so begin to think simple dog discipline rather than how complicated things can be made. Don't allow your dog to do something which you are going to forbid at a later date; the action is either acceptable or it is not. Whatever your dog is allowed to do it must understand that it is only being allowed, that it cannot take it for granted. First and foremost teach good manners; without these, a dog is presumptuous. It is not what a dog is allowed to do that is important, but how it sees its position in the pack and the respect it has for its leader and whether this makes it biddable. I have seen many dogs that have been made to follow all the complicated rules of feeding, keeping off furniture and not climbing the 'dominant making' staircase, still pull on the lead, bark and be generally bad mannered. I have also seen dogs that sleep upstairs, are not restricted to eating after the humans and share the settee of an evening with their owner be relied upon to keep their good manners and their respect. Keep the rules simple; keep training simple. Think from the dog's point of view and training can be fun.

Establishing the Rules

The first few weeks are important for noise sensitivity and socialization, so introduce your puppy to as much as possible but first make sure it knows who you are! If you are not pack leader it will have no one to trust. Make your own house rules. It is your dog and your home, but make sure the rules are sensible and easy for your dog to understand and above all be consistent. Don't negotiate on teaching the basic commands as they could be the difference between a well-behaved dog and an accident at a later date. A collie has a sense of humour and is naturally inquisitive, so the sooner you establish the basics and who is in charge the sooner it can 'free think' and you can enjoy its humour.

CHAPTER 7

Training is Fun

Once the basic good manners of puppy-hood are established you can start to stretch your youngster's capabilities and vocabulary. Learning, like good manners, is ongoing. It should never really start and it never really ends, and should not be confused with training. Learning is the process of understanding new things, working them out and thinking them through, whereas training is the education necessary for the dog to be able to learn to the best of its ability.

If we take the command to 'lie down' and look at it from a training point of view the dog must learn to lie down when it is told – this is training. If the dog sees something it is not sure of, something that puzzles it, if it has been taught to have thinking time it will use the lie down to work out the situation – this is learning. A dog maturing in an all-dog environment will learn by experience and its instincts will guide its curiosity. A dog maturing in a human environ-ment has all the natural dog instincts and is capable of working things out if the human element will allow it the time to do so. A dog's natural reactions to many situations are very fast; the move-ment of a cat will bring a spontaneous reaction with the instinct of the predator clicking into gear almost faster than a breath could be drawn. However, the same dog can spend one or more hours tracking down and studying the move-ment pattern of a mole; it is using its brain to work out a situation and will happily concentrate on the job in hand until it either reaches a conclusion or discovers another and better challenge. Once again, the natural instincts and behaviour of the dog are explaining how best we can train it. We just have to make the effort to learn to understand the dog's reactions and capabilities, and to resist the temptation to think for it.

Human beings often have preconceived ideas of how dogs should behave and have certain expectations for the dog in their life. Unfortunately, not all dogs are capable of living up to these expectations, or more often the expectations are not a problem but the way they are explained is, and the dog's right to a say in its own life is forgotten! A Border Collie is a thinking dog, and although I am willing to listen to many different theories no one will be able to convince me otherwise. An intelligent Border Collie can work things out for itself and can often put forward a good and valid argument to a human being who is prepared to listen – I call this thinking!

An example of the way a collie can work things out and put forward its argu-ment or point of view can be seen in the following account. Pip is a sheepdog and can work to a high standard, he is bidd-able and teaches novice handlers the skills of shepherding. If a handler gives

Border Collies have a remarkable ability for concentration and the more they are encouraged to think without becoming over-excited the more they will use their brain. Skye is moving in very stealthily as she stalks Tia.

Skye will stand in this position for as long as it takes to get a reaction.

Front view shows the power of the eye whilst Skye focuses totally on her subject but still allows Tia to move out of fight and flight distance (see Chapter 9).

Tia has moved away from the gaze and Skye is content that the game went her way. This whole event took fifteen minutes!

a command that is obviously wrong Pip will refuse to move; if the handler does not realize the dog is refusing for a reason he will repeat the command. At this point, Pip will lean in the correct direction, 'talking' to the handler with his body language. If the handler still refuses to 'listen' to him, Pip will cast a glance in my direction with a look of disdain. If no one makes a decision he will do what is correct and then return to base to await further instructions, but he will have to be persuaded to continue being patient with a human who refuses to 'talk' to him. If the novice handler still does not try to understand the dog he will fail to establish an empathy with it, but if the handler tries hard to communicate then the dog will begin to work with rather than against him.

The Border Collie is popular for its intelligence, its versatility and its ability to adapt, but these qualities also make it quick-witted, crafty and dare I say humorous to the point of being sarcastic! The collie's ability to be able to assess a situation and turn it to its own advantage has often left confused and mesmerized owners feeling that they are standing at the wrong end of the dog lead! It does not take long for a well-trained human to learn to walk a little faster in order to make it appear that their dog is not pulling on the lead. It's not hard to teach a human to give the dog permission to break the 'stay' command at the dog's wishes rather than their own: 'Just a little twitch of my shoulder, master, and a threat of moving and you are sure to give permission because you don't really want a confrontation just now.' Clever little dogs, but we have to admire their cheek!

Using Your Dog's Intelligence

It does not make sense to waste time and energy trying to *make* a collie work for you; it is far more enjoyable if it *wants* to work for you. So training is encouraging the dog to use its intelligence for your ends rather than its own. What you are training for is irrelevant, for the event is merely an extension of the foundation, for example training for sheepwork, agility, obedience or for a companion all require a good solid foundation with the same physical and mental boundaries, that of pack law. When the dog understands the rules and is biddable the handler can diversify into any of the above extensions.

I like to consider training as a game. Sometimes the handler is in the game and sometimes observing, sometimes the dog is in the game and at times it will observe. The concept of play and games in dog training is common but the equipment is usually toys and treats, when all that is really needed for the dog's attention is the handler.

Training is education and a dog cannot learn if it is in a state of high excitement or semi-hysteria, nor will it use its brain for thinking clearly if it is constantly expecting or looking for titbits. It does not need intelligence for a dog to work out that a certain action receives a food reward, so titbits are not making the dog use its brain. But intelligence is used for the dog to work out that it does not get to stage two unless stage one is completed. For example, a dog constantly being rewarded for coming back to heel will keep pulling for the reward and will still get from A to B in the usual time. A dog who is not allowed to travel forward

One twitch of the shoulder and flick of the ear told the author that Hope was not going to stay. A similar kind of human movement but in opposition and the ears go back in acknowledgement with a slight wag of the tail and Hope stays where he is told. Prevention is better than cure.

until it takes the correct position in the pack will work out that it is not going to reach B unless it adheres to pack rules, whereupon it will receive praise for being a valuable pack member. This is making the dog utilize its intelligence *for* the handler rather than against.

Pip using his body language to explain to the novice handler which way he should be going is exactly the same way that a dog learning the basics of obedience will communicate its intentions to its handler. If a dog is asked to stay in either a sit or down position it will give some indication of disobedience or misunderstanding before actually moving forward, and it is at this point the handler must 'read' the dog's language and intervene. It will be a very slight movement,

a drop of the shoulder, a twitch of the ear or maybe just a sideways glance, but this is the time to remind the dog that it must stay. If it moves forward it has committed itself to, and has achieved, a forward movement. If this happens and the handler repeats the command, allowing the dog to keep control of the ground it has just moved on to, then the handler loses credibility as a pack leader in this instance. If the dog is made to go back to the original position the handler is reclaiming control. If the handler 'reads' the dog correctly and intercepts the thought of forward movement before it is put into action then this rule of the game is easy for the dog to understand. This example is the basis for all the foundation rules and is not difficult to understand;

the difficulty is in being patient enough to learn to 'listen' to the dog's intentions. Human beings are always in a hurry and if the dog is told to stay and it appears it may be about to move, it is far easier to agree with the dog, or to negotiate by allowing it to keep the ground it has just occupied. There should be no negotiation with the important basics and good manners. Just a little effort and plenty of patience in the first few moments will make training much easier in the long run and will also make clear to your dog your intentions of being in control.

Titbits and toys should not be part of your quality time and a walk should not be reliant on methods of diversion for control. Hope is concentrating on a human being not a toy, and is therefore able to read that human being's body language.

There is a time for a dog to play and amuse itself – free time, and there is a time for a dog to learn – education. It is similar to a child going to school, in that if there has been no preparation for the time of learning in school the child will find it hard to settle. However, if during each day there has already been some form of education then the child will not be distressed by the demands of a formal education.

Enjoying a Walk

Walking is not just a means of exercise for the dog; it should also be a time of getting to know each other, of learning physical boundaries and of education. If handler and dog set off for a walk and the dog is pulling on the lead there will be few pleasantries passed between them, for the time will be spent arguing about leadership until the handler is in a position to let the dog loose. At this point the dog has pulled until it is convinced it is in control and so what better way to amuse itself when this cumbersome lead is taken off than to run as far as possible, sniffing the ground and ignoring the tiresome person who keeps calling to it. The handler has opted for the easy way by allowing the dog freedom when it has done nothing to deserve it!

How to make the walk fun and how to occupy the dog is not down to using up masses of energy, it is down to making the dog think. If you are willing to walk your dog miles each day you will be building up an athlete; Border Collies are athletic without special training. One of the most distressing scenarios is of the dog fed on high-energy food. The energy commands plenty of exercise, the exercise produces fitness and stamina which in turn demand more exercise, and the owner is concerned for the dog, which appears to be losing weight (usually due to nervous energy), and therefore increases the volume of the feed. Border Collies need exercise, but they also need their minds exercised, so walking a collie for two hours morning and night will not satisfy its inquisitive mind. It will merely make it fit enough to keep awake longer to be more demanding. If walking miles each day is costing both time and energy that you can ill afford then establish a different regime. A nice brisk walk coupled with training and some fun with mind games will mean that you will return with a collie who has been thoroughly exercised both bodily and mentally.

The walk should begin with good manners. If you are going by car to a suitable walking area then your dog should observe the courtesy of waiting to be asked to enter the car, sitting quietly during travelling and waiting to be asked out of the car. If your dog has been educated in the ways of your pack from the beginning this will not pose a problem. The beginning of the walk should be spent with your dog walking in the pack area that you have designated to him. If you allow your dog to run free immediately he will always anticipate freedom at the start of a walk. Instead, you should decide when your dog's free time starts, and when you unfasten the lead make your dog wait for several seconds before he wanders off on his own, all the time stroking and talking to him. A dog suddenly released will grab his freedom and run, inspired by the energetic release, whereas a dog released casually will take his free time casually.

As a puppy he will never be far away from you, and there is no reason for this to change as he matures, as he should always be looking to you for any possible change in the pack direction.

If we go back to the life of a puppy in the pack we will learn the behaviour expected of a human being if it is to become the pack leader. A litter of puppies may play at the pack perimeter but if they attempt to wander too far they will be severely reprimanded by the pack leader; likewise a group of Indian children playing too far from the perimeter of the camp will be reprimanded by the Big Chief. These leaders are not only looking after the youngsters who are very vulnerable, they are also looking after themselves. A group of youngsters may gather confidence as they grow and once they are outside of pack jurisdiction they can become insubordinate, forming a pack of their own, a smaller pack but tiresome and in need of being dealt with!

The human who allows the pack (the dog) to travel too far from the pack area before leadership has been established runs the risk of the pack (dog) becoming insubordinate. Some of the problems with the dog that has no physical boundaries are refusing to come back when called, running to other dogs and people, showing aggression to other dogs and barking. If the dog is allowed to keep extending its limits it will become responsible for itself and will make decisions that should only be made by a pack leader. This will lead the dog to believe it can take whatever course of action it likes. Also, if the dog is not of leader material and is not dominant it will feel the need to show aggression (born of nerves and insecurity) to any dog in the vicinity in the hope that the image of strength will protect it. Needless to say, the natural leader will show dominance of a different type and a fight may ensue.

It is important to establish your pack boundaries at an early age so as to ensure that your dog is always aware of your presence. The answer once again comes from the rule of the pack; you must make sure that your dog respects the area that belongs to you and does not leave pack jurisdiction without permission to do so. Imagine a line being drawn across the centre of a circle with you stood in the centre; the area immediately behind you is the area the dog should occupy when on a lead or loose with restricted freedom. The area in front of you is your space and your dog should only enter this on invitation. If your dog is off the lead, has more freedom, but your space (the area in front)

is not free to run in, the larger space behind you is the area your dog must be contained in. If the area in front is acceptable then your dog may be invited to run free in that area. Remember that your dog's place is directly behind you; this gives restricted freedom and equals total control. The immediate circle around you is the area of controlled freedom and equals close control. The area in the larger circle is freedom and equals control. The area outside pack jurisdiction is total freedom and equals distance control. The pack area need not be more than 25 yd (23 m) and your dog should not be allowed outside that area unless you are the established pack leader and you have complete distance control.

If you establish these rules when your dog is a puppy you should not encounter

Maureen asks Gemma and Floss to wait before they jump out of the car.

The car does not belong to the dogs so they wait for permission to jump back in.

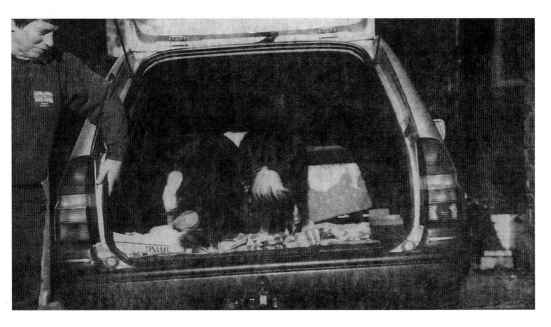

A tail end!

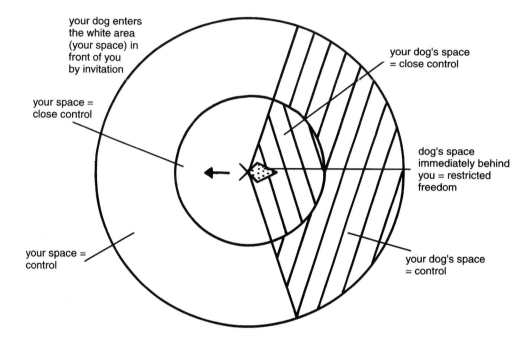

This is your 'pack area'. It must be no larger in radius than the distance you can command your dog, but should be approximately 20–25yd (18–23m). You are walking forwards into your own space (the white area). The dotted area immediately behind you is your dog's space providing restricted freedom. The smaller circle around you is an area of close control, the large circle is one of control and outside the circle is distance control. Your dog should be happy to walk or play in the shaded areas under your protection until such time as the white area, which is your space, is free and you have invited him to enter.

anything more than an occasional 'testing of your intentions', quite normal for a collie! Each time your puppy approaches the pack perimeter check it with your voice and get its attention. You can either call it back, change direction to encourage the puppy to follow on or, if it is happy to stay within the boundary, allow it to carry on and amuse itself. Keep giving your puppy a recall, make sure it comes back to your feet, make a fuss and allow it to carry on with its life. The recall must be happy, which it cannot be if the owner is calling and getting frustrated

and the puppy is expecting to be chastised. It is important it learns at an early age to respond to the first recall, as only when this is established can your youngster have total freedom.

Reward Training

Excellent idea but it is not new; responsible, caring owners have always rewarded their dogs. Titbits, now there's a new idea! Your dog should not be coming back to you because you are going to give a food reward, it should be coming back because it loves and respects you. If you are relying on titbits to recall your dog and the dog or rabbit it has just set off to chase outweighs the titbit in popularity then you may as well stop shouting! But if your dog respects you as pack leader, and you have an empathy with each other, not coming back does not enter into the equation. Titbits are fine in the correct context, as a treat. They can be given at the end of training, at bedtime, or just because you want to, but never to bribe, for this is what it is when food is used to 'persuade' a dog to conform to basic good manners.

So you do not need to take either titbits or toys on your walk – you are the most important thing in your dog's life and it will be happy to listen to what you have to say and to talk back to you if you are patient enough to communicate. If you do decide to take something to play with then make it into an interesting game, for example ball throwing can be good fun if it is used to make your dog think. Throwing a ball for your dog to retrieve is fine, once or maybe twice, but to keep throwing it can soon become a lazy form of exercise and, to an intelligent dog, is not very stimulating. The dog knows when it gives back the ball you are going to throw it again and it is soon waving its tail like a flag, jumping up and even running backwards in an effort to catch the ball in flight. Hold the ball in one hand, put it behind your back and change hands; ask your dog which hand the ball is in. Make it seek sensibly, it doesn't need to be encouraged with an excited voice for it will not be able to 'work', instead it will begin to get overexcited and may even begin to bark. Ask it quietly and if it doesn't understand the

game show it the ball and then repeat the action. The dog will soon decide where the ball is and will be surprised if it is wrong – you are both in the game. It will begin to work it out for itself but more importantly it will keep giving you its attention to see what you are going to do next. Now the ball is being used to make the dog think and can have a completely different effect on it and on its attitude to you – instead of the ball being the key to entertainment you are the key to making the ball stretch the dog's line of thinking.

One of my favourite pastimes is putting the 'bubble' over the dog's head. Hope could be thinking any one of a number of things but we can still have a 'conversation' about his thoughts.

Don't just do a 'stay' while you are in front of your dog. Pip is used to sitting still whilst someone is both walking and running around him in circles.

Make your dog sit and stay and walk several yards ahead of it – your dog is out of the game. Hide the ball in the grass or amongst some leaves, making it easy for your dog to find the first time. Ask your dog to find the ball and, until it understands the game, help it to seek – you are both in the game. When your dog understands the game it will seek on its own and you can observe – you are not in the game.

During this time you may have covered quite some distance on your walk but, instead of both you and your dog 'doing your own thing' or you repeatedly throwing a ball, you and your dog will have been *communicating*. Your dog will not have had time to run around selecting new areas to investigate and sniff, it will have been engrossed in you and what you have to offer. And what you have to offer is you with a toy to make mind games, not a toy to make a mindless game! Your dog will appreciate you and will be looking forward to everything you do with it, for you will be rapidly becoming interesting; you are also in control. You have the ball, you start the game, you hide it, and you dictate who is in the game and when. If you want to give your dog a treat at the end of the game you can give it a titbit, but it is not necessary and is a better treat if it comes once, at the end of the walk or on arrival home. You will find if you give your dog titbits during the game or the walk it will begin to search for the treats, and the lure of food will cause excitement, which is hardly beneficial to thinking!

Take Pip as an example again. He shakes paws with people he meets, it is his way of saying hello without any fuss and he does it if he is asked to; afterwards he receives a pat and a 'good boy', then off he goes happy with his day. If he is given a treat (and some people have given him a titbit for the paw, causing me to frown and Pip's brain to disengage), he begins to expect a treat each time he provides a paw. Soon he is bartering for food using the 'shake my paw' as his bribe. He is dictating who should do what and when, which is neither good mannered nor necessary for he is quite happy to shake paws and equally happy to carry on about his business. He likes using his brain, he likes communicating, he likes to work and he is not bad mannered, so why complicate his education with something humans may be able to relate to but which dogs see in a totally different context?

Make your walk part of a training session. Border Collies are greedy for information so make sure you are the one to provide it; if you don't, they will find their own and before long they will be into mischief. Only part of the reason for walking is exercise. The other is quality time and communication, getting to know one another, for no matter how well you think you know your dog it will be constantly surprising you, so make sure you are always striving to keep on the same wavelength. You need to strike a happy medium and only you can decide what that is, so it is essential you understand your dog's motives and that you have certain rules. The rules are not just for your dog's benefit but for yours also. There is little point in making sure your dog heeds a rule one day if you have forgotten it exists the next. You both need free time, you to think or talk to someone you meet and your dog to enjoy all the new smells and to explore the surrounding area. But this time is designated by you – don't allow your dog to pull you onto the grass verge just because it feels like checking out the local perfumery. Granted your dog may want to check out the area, but who is he to decide that you have not some plans of your own at that moment? Make him wait a second and then when *you* are ready let him have his fun. Enjoy some free time just walking together (both out of the game) and then bring his attention back on to you. Try calling him while you are partially hidden from sight (not completely, as he doesn't understand the game yet and will never enjoy it if it induces panic); now you are introducing a different game of hide and seek. Alter your pace when he is walking with you so that you are walking 'slow', 'fast', 'faster' and maybe

even 'jog'. Make sure his pace alters to suit yours and then introduce the word sound (for example, 'walk') that he can associate to the pace. Change direction when he least expects it and enjoy the expressions on his face as he tries to figure out what you are going to do next. I don't advise using changing direction as a method of teaching heel walking, as most collies are clever enough to be one jump in front of you, hence the reason why it makes an excellent game. One of my favourite pastimes is 'putting the bubble over the dog's head', that is, trying to imagine what your dog is saying and having a 'conversation' with him. If you do something which causes a puzzled expression when he looks at you, imagine what he might be saying to you and answer him back. It is all part of enjoying your dog and having fun, but be careful there is no one around to hear you or you may find yourself receiving some strange looks from fellow humans! Not all dogs like all of the games so it is up to you to think of ways to 'work' and play with your dog, to find methods it will like and to explore all the possibilities together.

Don't wait for your dog to be disobedient on a walk and then begin to train it – prevention is better than cure. Use your private space to teach basic control. The garden, yard or garage are all quiet places where you can train and arrange distractions to test your control. You do not need any complicated training; this comes later if you decide to take training a stage further. All you need to begin with are the basic commands – sit, down, stay, wait, recall. You don't even need to be concerned if your dog appears to have an aversion to sitting, as it is not the most natural position for a collie and many prefer to lie down. All you need to be concerned with to begin training is being able to make your dog stop when you want. Concern yourself with other positions at a later date. If you have done the basics from puppyhood, most of these commands will be part of your dog's everyday vocabulary and you will now be making sure you can retain control when there are distractions. Ask your dog to stay and then walk around it in a circle; this will get it used to you moving positions without it following you. Keep making the circle larger and gradually introduce more movement. When your dog remains in the 'stay' while you are jumping up and down and waving your arms (I advise total privacy for this exercise!), you are ready to move on to the next stage. Now try to make your dog stay while someone else enters the game, someone who may talk to you or move around, someone your dog would really love to go to. Use the same method for pack position, just you and your dog on your own territory with your dog walking behind you, and when you are satisfied you have control introduce a third party to the 'game'. Once again, don't fall into the trap of using bribes. If you are walking your dog on the pavement and it rushes off to meet someone on the other side of the road you may not have a distraction available and even if you have it just might not be interesting enough. Negotiating the basics can cause an accident! If your dog loses concentration during training it is ceasing to focus, whereas a dog can in fact focus on its prey for hours – it will hold its attention on to something which interests it. Value yourself higher than a toy or a titbit, your dog needs to focus on you!

When you are teaching your dog the English language remember that to him these are just sounds. If you keep this in your mind it will make word association easier and will prevent you from confusing your dog. The sound 'down' will probably be the word you use for making your dog lie down, but if the sound is to be associated with the action it cannot also be used to make the dog go down when it has jumped up. This must be a different sound, for example 'off' or 'no'. The latter is an excellent command, for you will have introduced this to your puppy almost from day one. It will associate this sound with a reversal of action – 'whatever I am doing is incorrect and the opposite is usually advisable'. Clever little dogs soon work out what 'no' means and the next command on the tip of your tongue is often seconds behind the action! If you tell your dog to 'stay' when you go to bed you are wasting a command for it will not be in the same place or position in the morning, so use a different sound. I use 'wait' to tell my dogs to wait outside or inside or in the car. A friend of mine uses a different sound for this situation and uses 'wait' to tell her dog there is a command about to come which will require concentration; when I am asking my dogs to concentrate I use 'listen'. It is not obligatory for you to use the same words as other people use – if you choose to introduce food sounds to your dog for commands, fish and chips, bacon and eggs, then that will be the language your dog will become accustomed to! Your concern is making sure that you, and anyone else who is concerned with your dog, are comfortable with the words you are using and that you avoid confusion. If you are going to training classes or are involved in any obedience where your dog is walking at the side of you, choose a different word to the one you will be using for total control. I make sure I can understand my commands so I keep them simple. I tell my dog to 'keep behind' for total control, and if this or a similar command was used you could then use 'heel' to bring your dog forward into the recognized obedience position. Just a little forethought and training can be made very simple and uncomplicated.

House Training with a Difference

If you have a spare five minutes don't spend it wondering what you would do if you won a fortune, for while you are dreaming of a new home your dog may be planning on demolishing your old one! You don't have to be outside to train your dog; in fact, some of the most interesting training games are based inside and because they are done in a relaxed atmosphere they are constructive in building a companionable relationship. Try to let your dog invent a game rather than dictate to him. Human beings are not always very convincing as pack leaders, yet they are often great at telling their dog what to play and how to play it. If you insist on throwing a ball and teaching your dog to retrieve it you are robbing him of the chance to use his brain and figure it out for himself. Besides, maybe he doesn't always want to bring it back to you; after all, it does seem a little silly to keep bringing back a ball that you insist on throwing away again! Maybe it is a rainy day and you have both had all the exercise you need given the weather conditions. Try sitting on the floor with your dog or puppy and just gently roll a ball towards it. If you keep rolling the ball without making an issue of what the dog should do, don't be surprised if it begins to roll it back to you. If it rolls it halfway back don't lean over and pick it up (the dog is making you play the game his way), ignore him until he rolls it right back to you. This game is excellent in the

Betty Duggan will play with Jem with a ball but if Jem decides she is tired of retrieving or if she becomes too excited (watch the tail) Betty will be guided by her dog and give her something else to think about.

If a dog is taught basic rules and then left to its own initiative it will invent its own games. Pip is not allowed to use his teeth on a ball but he will play for hours on his own with a football just rolling it gently round or pushing it up a wall and watching it roll back down.

garden with a football. The dog is not allowed to nip the ball but it is allowed to roll it (it will learn this inside with the small ball), and before long you have got a potential football player, and no burst balls.

Try placing three containers on the floor and put a small ball or toy under one, let the dog see it and then shuffle them. Can your dog work out where the object is? The same object can be hidden under a paper or chair and the dog can 'seek' it, but always make sure your dog is thinking and not acting foolishly and make sure you organize when and where these sessions take place. When you have finished give your dog a 'break' or 'finish' signal, which means the session is finished and he does not continue with any of these games on his own. Also, at the end of any training or game make your dog sit quietly in his bed or on his own 'space' so that he can settle and have some thinking time on his own.

A dog is being demanding if it brings something to you in search of attention; it may be a lead or a toy or a paper and it will be insistent you take it. At some time it will have brought you something and received attention so it will have stored this information in its mind, that producing an item gains attention. Neither is it being an amazing mind-reader if it just happens to pick up the very article you had already thought of reaching for; it will have read your body language and will have presumed it could intervene. There are times when this behaviour is both amusing and acceptable; after all, your dog would not be a Border Collie if it was not both cheeky and humorous, but you have to decide if the action was cheeky or bad mannered. Often in the young dog it is bad mannered and if allowed to go unchecked the humour of the situation will not be able to be appreciated as the dog matures, for its manners will always be in question. There is a time to play and test your patience and be a little cheeky and a time to be respectful and good mannered. Your dog has to earn this freedom and it cannot learn if you do not teach it.

There is no age limit for educational games. Puppies can begin learning and old dogs can have fun teasing you as they make their own rules to the games. There is nothing difficult in this kind of education and it is not dependent on wide open spaces or good weather, and neither will you have any need to bribe your dog into good behaviour or to keep producing a never-ending supply of toys. All you need is yourself, your dog and a little imagination and you are on your way to having a companionable relationship with each other.

Making Training Fun

Don't rely on titbits and toys to train your dog, it should be focused on you. Concentrate on building a companionable relationship and on making training fun without making your dog hysterical. Your dog is learning all the time and even when you think you have finished training it is still absorbing information.

Always allow time for your dog to have its own, quality time. Make a walk interesting and keep communicating with each other.

CHAPTER 8

The Adolescent or Older Dog

There is no such thing as the perfect dog or trainer. All handlers make mistakes and dogs are always quick to notice inconsistency, no matter how slight, and will take advantage of it. You *can* teach an old dog new tricks, but unfortunately human beings far too often become set in *their* ways, often failing to see that they too can still learn and they can learn from their dog! Even the most conscientious owner, who has spent time and patience with their puppy, can still find they have a wayward adolescent to cope with when the dog reaches the one-year-old mark. However, if the foundation has been designed to be solid and the subsequent building (training) has been done with care, there should be a sufficient understanding between dog and handler for the problems to be of little consequence. But the older dog or rescue entering your home can cause a new set of problems and, unfortunately, even if there is a foundation to fall back on (and this will be unlikely), you will not be aware of it. In fact, it is far more likely that the dog's past will be harbouring the roots to its problems and you will not be in possession of the key to release the information that can make training or rehabilitation so much easier.

You may have a wayward youngster, an older dog or a rescue, but if there are problems there is always a similar pattern; pulling on the lead, poor recall, lacking in concentration, no focus on the handler, chasing cars, chasing birds, fixed staring. If these problems are not addressed the scenario can become quite alarming, resulting in destruction, nipping, running away, aggression to other dogs and aggression to people, with the added concern of the dog threatening or showing aggression to the owner.

A bad-mannered dog is not a pleasure to be with and one that shows no respect for its owner rapidly becomes a problem. Unfortunately, help for this kind of dog is not always readily available, for fashion dictates that it is inevitable that Border Collies follow certain traits and this must be accepted. I call it the 'Border Collies Do' fashion – Border Collies do chase, do destruct, do pull, do nip. These condemnations are in themselves destructive to the breed, for Border Collies *don't*. It is all down to management!

I believe there is no such thing as a bad dog. Dogs with problems are either the result of bad management or bad breeding and both of these are down to human error. In the case of bad breeding I feel there is no excuse. The future of the Border Collie is dependent on good breeding and of breeding true to type. If a dog is genetically unsound then the breeder must shoulder the responsibility. The most conscientious of breeders can produce a throwback, but if the correct research has been done in most cases the result is not serious and may only be a throwback in colour. If the problem is more serious then the homework was probably not very thorough. In defence of good breeders, it is heartbreaking to produce a quality puppy and to find out that the new owner who came with references really knows nothing about dogs at all. Or worse, the references were fine but the new owner prefers not to take on board all the advice which has been given (and no one else will know the line better than the breeder) and then complains because the puppy has become wayward.

The best-bred dog with a solid foundation cannot help but suffer if it is subjected to cruelty and unfortunately it is a sad fact that rescue kennels are full of dogs of all breeds which have been abused or abandoned. At the time of writing, the number of Border Collies suffering from neglect or abuse and in need of caring homes is at an all-time high. The intelligence and loyalty of the breed have made it popular in all walks of life, but its versatility and adaptability have introduced it into some areas where it can only suffer. Far too many are in homes where they are misunderstood. In some cases the owners have no intention of adapting to the needs of their dog, while in other instances the owners are trying so hard to give their dogs the understanding they think they need that they have become bogged down by training aids. The owners are employing methods such as choke chains, water squirters, rolled-up newspapers, scruffing, or so many titbits the dog is in danger of becoming obese. A suitcase is needed to make sure all the necessary aids are to hand when needed!

If your problem is with a young dog you have either bred yourself or purchased as a puppy, you will be able to trace its history and maybe the reason for the breakdown in communication will be evident. If your dog is a rescue or has been rehomed with you for whatever reason, unless you have its history you will have to do some detective work into its mind.

To begin with, you need to recognize the type of dog you have. Is it smooth-coated or long, are its ears pricked, does it have soft or sharp eyes? From the previous chapters we can presume that a prick-eared, short-coated dog may be genetically more energetic than its longer coated cousin. Is it nervous? If so, does it appear to be frightened or just shy? Is there any sign of aggression, and if so is it dominant or nervous aggression? When you have recognized some of your dog's characteristics and its temperament you are on the way to finding the reason for the problems.

The first line of investigation is diet. Is the dog full of energy or hyperactive? If so, you may need to consider the energy level you are feeding. If it is a home-reared youngster who is suffering from 'adolescent syndrome', what did you feed it on as a puppy and for how long? If you did not rear the dog, can you find out any dietary history? If not, it might be as well to presume it needs to be on a lower energy level. Is the dog registered with the ISDS or the KC? If so, you will be able to research its pedigree and find out if there are any obvious genetical defects or problems.

Now the picture of the dog's background should be a little clearer and you can start to address the problems. The foundation for training explained in the earlier chapters needs to be strong and firm. If there are flaws in the foundation (and there must be or there would not be a problem), then the building must be taken back to the foundation; in other words you must take your training back to basics. The advantage of training the home-reared dog which has problems is that you know the dog's background, but unfortunately it also means the dog has had its own way within your pack for a long time and has probably assumed leadership. No leader takes kindly to being demoted. The newcomer to your home may not provide the advantage of background knowledge but neither does it know your 'territory'. If you assume the role of leader from day one the dog will not only accept your leadership but it will also find strength in you, enabling it to be able to trust humans sooner rather than later.

If there is one obvious problem in your dog's behaviour there will more than likely be several more which have not yet materialized, or that you haven't noticed. If one brick is missing from a wall the chances are that the position of the other bricks in the wall will be affected, causing a weak structure. For example, a dog pulling on a lead is a problem but why is it pulling? It obviously sees itself as in control on the walk, so it will no doubt be in charge in other areas of its owner's life; it may be subtle but it will be there. There are training aids for all kinds of problems and lead walking is no exception, from a harness to a head collar and of course the collie's nightmare, the choke chain. It's rather like putting a muzzle on an aggressive dog and saying 'my dog used to bite but it's alright now'. It's still the same dog with the same attitude, it just can't do it whilst it is muzzled. The whole aspect of training needs to be addressed and not just the immediate problem.

Lead Walking

The lead-walking problem is not hard to solve if the owner understands it from the dog's point of view. The dog is taking command and assuming leadership, but the owner has inadvertently encouraged it to believe it is the leader. We all like to think our dogs are clever so when you go to put on the shoes and coat you keep for taking your dog for a walk, you will probably admire your dog's quick thinking when it goes to pick up its own lead. Or maybe you pick up the lead and your dog becomes excited and runs to the door. Either way, by the time you reach the door your dog is already jittery with excitement about the coming walk. But what right has your dog to presume you are going to take it for a walk because you happen to pick up *your* lead and put on *your* clothes? When he was young, you may have encouraged him to 'fetch' the lead or said 'Where are we going?' or 'Are you ready?'. There is no reason why you should not encourage your dog to look forward to the walk, but he should not *expect* you to take him. The difference is subtle but your dog must realize that you are in charge and if you were to pick up the lead, move it, then put it down again he has no right to create a scene because things did not go his way. Also when you are taking him for a walk he should show his enthusiasm, wait for you to be ready and then wait while you go out of the door first. Now you are starting out in control of the situation.

Perhaps you do not allow your dog to dictate the first few steps of the walk, so why does he still pull? What do you do on the rest of the walk? If you always go the same way it may not seem to matter if your dog goes ahead, but to him he is telling you that you will follow him to his usual place. When you take the lead off does he wait to be given permission to run free or does he just grab his freedom and shove off? When he is running free how far does he go, does he take notice of you, or does he only come back when he is ready? Unless you can honestly say that your dog comes back first time, even when there are distractions, does not run too far away from you, and is always interested in what you are doing, even in his free time, then the dog is in charge by way of you allowing it!

Think about the basic pack rules, the youngsters (or untrained) members of the pack do not leave pack jurisdiction until they understand and respect the rules of pack and the pack leader. If you allow your youngster to wander too far too soon he will make his own decisions. Many Border Collies are 'conditioned trained'; they are educated to behave in a certain manner in a given situation. For example, many owners who attend training classes with their dogs complain that although their dog is well-behaved in class and doesn't pull on the lead or misbehave, it is a monster on the way home and during the rest of the week. This dog is trained to behave in class, but the owner has failed to make the dog respect him outside the class. Similarly, I have seen Border Collies win in the obedience ring and then proceed to pull

their owner back to the car. They are trained to do certain actions in certain familiar surroundings. Let us return to Pip again. He has done television work and a number of photo shoots and he is normally a very active little chap. If a camera is pointed at him and he is asked to wait he will pose for far longer than he would normally remain still with nothing to watch or do. He is conditioned or educated to do this; he is also a great show-off and while he is posing he is receiving attention. The dog in the class and the dog in the ring are both receiving attention and the owner's attitude will change when he leaves the training or competitive area. This endorses the fact to the dog that it does not have to respond the same way towards its owner away from this education or conditioning.

The principles of pack position in relation to dog and handler are important. You must be the leader and your dog should become your pack, but you cannot become a very convincing leader if your dog is always in front of you. As described in our earlier training chapter your dog's space is behind you and your space is in front of you, and your dog should not presume it can enter your space unless you have given it permission to do so. If your dog is walking at your side with its shoulder level with your knee and its head in front of you then it is assuming the role of leader; it is in front of you. Could you imagine the Indian Chief riding half a pony length behind his braves, or the Army General being content to follow his men whilst trying to remain in command?

Many of the modern training methods follow fashion and with a breed as quick-witted as the Border Collie these methods often provide the excuse for the

Floss is pulling and assuming the role of leader.

Floss is being taught she must stay behind in her own space and not move forwards until given permission.

Floss is given permission to move forwards but she must remain in her own space and not move level with her handler. The handler's body language is 'talking' to the dog.

The handler is now able to stride forwards and her body language is more relaxed, Floss is in a position where she can see all that is going on ahead but is still in her pack position.

Off the lead and handler and dog can now walk for miles together. Floss can be invited into her leader's space at any time.

When your dog recognizes its space is behind you and you can walk without having to keep reminding it you can then invite it forwards to any position you choose. Floss is demonstrating heelwork for competition obedience.

dog to work the owner! If you are training for competition work you will probably need your dog to walk slightly in front and to turn its head and look up at you. The dog that has been taught to walk behind you will find no problem in entering your space and learning how to walk for the purpose of competing. As far as I am aware there is no rule stating a dog must walk in this manner in the ring, but it is fashionable and therefore will attract the judge's eye. From the dog's point of view this is preventing it from walking naturally, as no dog would normally walk with its head twisted round and it is contradictory to place it in front of its leader and then insist it turns to look at him. The theory is that the dog is being made to concentrate on its handler, but both guide dogs and sheepdogs disprove this theory! If you can understand how the dog relates to this positioning and how competition is not the same as basic good manners you will be able to separate the two.

Now try to lead-walk your dog while studying your actions and your dog's reactions very carefully. If your dog goes in front and pulls on the lead, and you say 'heel' and pull it back into place how does your dog see it? If I were the dog I would think that you were allowing me to go in front – that's nice, I get there sooner and I'm in control – but then you pull me back and say a sound of 'heel', and sometimes I get a pat and sometimes I get a titbit, I might even get a toy dangling in front of my nose. Whatever happens, I won't get the sound or the pat or the titbit until I have done what I want, which is to pull my owner on behind me! This is the way the dog sees it and this is endorsed by the number of dogs who pull on the lead but walk better

off it (they are conditioned to pull on the lead). Also, these dogs will walk behind me when I insist and I introduce another sound, but when they go back to their owners they pull as soon as they hear the 'heel' sound.

The pack leader does not educate his pack by constantly bringing it back; it is not allowed to go forward! So reverse the situation by asking your dog to sit and wait behind you while you walk forwards into your space. Now ask your dog to follow slowly, using only the available space behind you. He is not allowed to pass your legs or try to enter your space. Your progress forward will be slow, but you are dealing with an intelligent dog and one that appreciates rules it can understand. It will not take long for your dog to realize it cannot take an advantage position and each time it tries it is made to sit and wait while you lengthen the leadership gap. If you weaken and allow him to take advantage he will get from A to B with some points to his credit, but if he is made to understand he does not get from A to B unless he does it your way he will soon settle into the new regime. It will not be necessary to keep making him; he will soon learn that if he slows down before he reaches your space he will be allowed to carry on with the walk. This method deals with more than one problem. It will teach your dog its correct pack position, it will be expected to sit at the *first* time of asking, and it will not be allowed to move from the 'wait' position until given permission. Your dog will also be expected to walk at your pace (never be tempted to quicken your pace to suit your dog). But more importantly you are constantly communicating with your dog and it is beginning to focus on you (if it doesn't and it prefers to sniff the grass verge, you will bring it back to order until it asks for permission). When you are walking you can give your dog permission to run free within your pack area. However, one word of warning – if your dog is used to the 'heel' sound and it associates this with walking in front or pulling, you will need to provide a different sound for your new 'game'. 'Behind' or 'back' are both comfortable words to use and 'heel' could be used to bring your dog forward.

What about the training aids? Great, if you want to run the risk of even more problems! The rolled-up newspaper can make an introvert dog nervous and an extrovert dog aggressive. The water squirter can have the same effect, but many collies love the water on them. The choke chain is an instrument of torture and is not even worth contemplating. If a dog cannot be controlled by its owner without being nipped, bullied, pulled and choked then it is time to look seriously into the relationship they have, and aiming to enhance that instead of using an aid which will either rob the dog of its pride or make it arrogant and defiant!

Chasing and Destruction

Chasing falls into one of the 'Border Collies Do' categories. Sadly, Border Collies who chase bring disrepute to the rest of their breed and through no fault of their own. It is so easy to blame the sheepdog instinct for chasing and destruction. I have talked to so many on the receiving end of such explanations and find it not only sad that this is the conclusion reached, but also that the owners concerned are left feeling that they have a dog they have no hope of controlling.

Sheepdogs should not be destructive and nor should they chase. The instinct that the shepherd nurtures in his dog is the gathering, herding instinct and the dog is encouraged to use its brain and the power of its eye, not its teeth, to move stock. If and when the sheepdog uses its teeth it should be on command and in a controlled manner. However, no dog is perfect and the best-trained sheepdog can lose its temper and 'grip' in a moment of thoughtlessness, but if the dog has been encouraged rather than discouraged to do this then the consequences could be severe.

Chasing and destruction are part of the same problem and are usually caused by the incorrect control of the instincts. Dogs are all pack animals and the basic wolf instinct lies dormant in most breeds, but if encouraged this instinct will rise to the surface and many owners encourage the wrong instincts without realizing what they are doing. For a pack of wolves or dogs to hunt successfully they need to be able to gather, herd, stalk, hypnotize, catch, outrun and kill. All members of a hunting party will be genetically capable of doing all the jobs needed but each will have its own task to perform, the one at which it excels. The Border Collie carries all the necessary genes to perform the job it is bred to do, but it will be better equipped for some of the tasks than for others. In the case of the sheepdog, if it has a strong tendency to grip this is curbed and the gathering (outrun) instinct is nurtured. If it shows too much eye it is discouraged from sitting at the field edge staring, and if it shows little eye it is encouraged to walk on to sheep with the handler to give it confidence. Sheepdog training is no different to training the companion collie. The companion dog is being trained for a different job, but it is still the same dog with the same instincts and intelligence and therefore the same degree of instinct control is necessary, albeit for different reasons.

If a puppy is allowed to destroy its surroundings it will grow up with no respect regarding what it can and can't use its teeth on. Its mother would have disciplined it in no uncertain terms if it had tried to play with her in the same way that it played with its litter mates. The puppy growing up with older dogs who have been allowed to retain their pack instincts within their own space will find it can only have so much freedom before the older members put it in its place. At no time will a puppy be allowed to use its teeth on another pack member except when playing educational games and these games are for the purpose of learning to hunt. The companion collie is far too often encouraged to use its teeth – it will shake a ball, play a tuggy game or tug on the lead with its teeth to obtain possessions. It will also have been encouraged to chase by running after balls, sticks, other dogs on a walk, birds; all these are bringing out the part of the instinct that is not really needed. A dog soon reaches hysteria if it is unable to catch its prey, so chasing things like birds, aeroplanes and cars often ends in barking, then the barking comes before the chase and sometimes instead of the chase. Cars can seem an easy prey, so the chase soon becomes addictive and obsessive, beginning with the thrill of the chase to the dog using its skills to stalk, hypnotize, chase and probably yap when the car disappears.

If you take your dog for a walk and it is chasing cars there is more than one problem. The dog is not focused on you and on pleasing you and it is not responsive to lead walking. So the long-term correction is to teach your dog to walk behind you, which will make your dog more aware of your presence and confirm to your dog that you are pack leader. In the short term you need to change your attitude and body language to your dog. If you are aware of a car in the vicinity you will probably show a change in your body tension, which will alert the dog that you are aware of the car and that, like him, you are showing a response to it. This is the first stage of your dog dictating to you! The simplest and fastest way of dealing with the situation is to ignore it; just keep walking, with your dog on a short lead, and do not give him time for the pleasure of even fixing his stare. While you are keeping him mobile, behind you and at your pace, you are firmly telling him to walk on, while your body language is turned away from the car (pack leader faces only when he is challenging). When you are past the car and your dog is out of the 'fight and flight' distance, tell him he is a good dog but keep on walking. If you stop and make a fuss of him at this point you are endorsing his belief that the car is an issue, but when he has settled back to a normal walk then you can give him more praise. If your dog's mind is committed to chasing the car and you issue praise immediately after the situation has subsided he may as well revert to this order each time. Only when your dog's mind is committed to walking sensibly can you praise him!

If you find it difficult to keep your dog mobile you will have to address the situation in a different manner. When you hear the car try to keep your body language unresponsive, make your dog lie down and make him stay still. You need to keep him as far from the edge of the road as possible and your body must be between him and the traffic – you are pack leader, therefore you stand between him and any threat. Don't pander to his imagination by telling him what a good boy he is; if he were, he would not be in this position! Keep him still and be firm but kind, and immediately the car is past walk in the opposite direction, denying your dog any opportunity to stare after the car and only praising him when his mind is committed to doing as you wish.

These are two proven methods of dealing with car chasers, and in each instance you are treating the dog with little importance. The more of an issue the chasing becomes and the more your body language shows signs of stress, the more the dog will enjoy it. If you are unresponsive, treat him with disdain and continue doing what you want, the chase will cease to be fun. However, this is only a short-term solution; the real correction lies in finding out why the dog believes it has the right to take over command in the first place. There is always more than one way to solve a problem, but no trainer can be a 'fly on the wall'. When you have learnt to understand your dog you will understand how to deal with any problems.

Chasing not only involves cars – unfortunately birds, bicycles and even other dogs can all become hyperactive entertainment and although they are not as difficult to deal with they are probably in evidence more often. Whereas cars will only be a problem on a walk and other dogs can always be avoided until your dog is more biddable, you may have to remove your dog from the temptation of birds flying overhead and bicycles passing the garden gate. If your dog is chasing birds it will probably have started on its own territory, in the garden or the yard, and will be a result of it finding its own amusement and a way of using up surplus energy. Once again, diet can play an important factor and the need to exercise the dog's mind, not just its body. A dog can spend hours in a garden and never chase birds if it has been educated to think.

Human beings prevent dogs from focusing on one thing by constantly supplying them with different ideas when the first one has not been thoroughly explored. If a puppy is provided with a supply of different toys and the owner is constantly playing games, using all the toys, the puppy grows up to be constantly searching for something different and is committed to always being on the go. This puppy then grows up never satisfied with its own company and never using its mind to full capacity. All dogs need a 'quiet time' and their own space to retire to. They do not *have* to have a huge supply of toys; in fact, they do not *have* to have toys at all! Toys are a human aid and the fact that most training advice states that a dog should only have one toy at a time questions the reason for a variety of toys. Boredom cannot come into the equation, for if a dog is mentally and physically exercised it will be happy to settle down and be peaceful. Boredom is a human trait, and we make the mistake of thinking that dogs become bored of the same food and bored with the same toy. The human being likes a variety of foods and therefore presumes the dog should be the same, but in the wild the dog's diet is not very varied, just meat from the kill and herbs from grazing. Originally, man lived with similar eating habits to the dog, meat from the kill and vegetation, and until quite recently our diet has continued to consist of mainly meat and vegetables. It has been during the latter half of the twentieth century that our palate has been introduced to a more varied diet with the advent of 'convenience foods' and 'take-outs', but whether or not this is advantageous is probably debatable. However, the fact remains that we often try to enforce our ideas of what our dogs need in relation to our own lives, rather than what the dog needs as a dog.

Recall

A dog that does not come back when it is called is not only bad mannered but dangerous. The runaway dog can cause a motor accident or a dogfight; it can be an embarrassment and can both annoy and frighten people who are not used to dogs, and a dog that does not come back at the first time of asking is a runaway dog. A dog that comes back 'usually' or 'when there are no distractions' does not have a recall; it understands to come back when it is ready and when there is not a better offer available. Age is not an excuse for a poor recall and neither is time, for a puppy should know no other than to come back and the older dog should not be given freedom outside its recall distance. The rules for the pack area for the older or problem dog are no different to the rules for training the younger dog or puppy that are described in Chapter 7, but this dog will not be as receptive. Teaching a recall is not difficult, but convincing the adolescent who you have reared from a puppy that the regime is about to change is not easy.

This youngster is not used to behaving with its owner and is not in the habit of coming when called. It may respond to a stranger or a dog trainer, but it will have a problem accepting this authority from the owner who has previously negotiated the recall. The dog entering your home as an older dog may have been used to negotiating with its previous owner or it may have had no training at all. Either way, if you begin as you mean to go on this dog could be easier than the rebellious teenager for he will understand his place in your pack from day one.

For the recall you will need a training aid, nothing complicated or expensive, just a rope clothes line or a length of sash cord. Tie knots in the rope at intervals to make handling easy, put a loop at your end and a lead clip on the other and you are ready to go. Begin in the garden by letting your dog realize the recall is a 'happy' command, because if the recall is not happy your dog has no reason to come back to you. Once again, you must look at your command from the dog's point of view. If when you recall your dog it does not come back but you continue calling, you are not explaining to your dog that the sound has any meaning other than to carry on doing what it is doing. If it comes back after several calls and you tell if off it will not want to come back to you next time, but if you ignore its bad manners you will be endorsing its behaviour. Apply the same pack area rules as in Chapter 7 and use the cord to let your dog know when he is nearing the edge of his physical boundary. A slight tug on the cord with a corresponding sound will show your dog the boundary and will give it a warning sound. Make sure the sound that you give for him to recognize is a sound (command) that you

A recall should be one of your dog's favourite commands and it should always come running to you on the first call. Hope is running at speed, all his weight is off the ground and his body language is happy.

Body language of both human and dog are totally relaxed and happy and as the dog nears its handler its forward motion is checked as it controls its speed.

The happy recall. There is little more satisfying than seeing this happy expression on a dog's face as it propels itself forwards with speed and grace for the sole intention of being near its human partner.

are comfortable with. Strange as it may seem, most of my dogs know that 'oy' means they have gone far enough – I know it is not a word, but neither can it be confused with any word and it is sharp enough for the dogs to take notice. Don't use your recall to make your dog stay within the boundary, for you are not recalling only keeping in contact and making sure that your dog is not so engrossed in his own affairs that he forgets you exist. Every so often do give a recall and make sure your dog comes straight back to you.

The mistakes usually made with a recall, even with a line, are calling more than once (usually habit), constant use of the dog's name, not making the dog come right back to base and not making the right sounds at the right time. To begin with, you have to assume that your dog does not understand the first recall, so it is no good waiting to see if he will come. Call his name to let him know he is in

the game and follow it immediately with your recall sound, making sure the tone is inviting but also commanding. Don't wait to see what his next move is for his body language will tell you immediately if he is going to come to you, and if he is responding keep him coming with gentle but encouraging praise. If his body language is not responsive bring him straight towards you with the cord. Do not praise him whilst the cord is in use. You do not want him to think that you *want* to use the cord, but as soon as he is at your feet give him the praise he would have got if he had come of his own accord. Don't ask him to sit in front of you after the recall, this presentation can be introduced later. You are bringing your dog back to your pack so welcome him to you and then before you give him another command ask him to come behind you ready for the next instruction, or more free time. This is easy training, it is fun and it is communication but

The author keeps in verbal contact with Skye to make sure she is always listening and to explain she must not go beyond the pack perimeter without permission.

remember not to keep using your dog's name for it is not a command. Once you have brought him into the game with his name he should not need to keep hearing it, especially if he is keeping focused on you. If his concentration is elsewhere use his name once to let him know the game is in progress. I use the term 'game' for in all training the dog is either responsive or not, and if not you have to make him want to be responsive. I also believe that training is fun, and if the dog enjoys it the training is made easier, but I don't believe in the use of toys for games or for distraction. I am the toy and I must be the attraction, I want my dog focused on me, wanting to know where I am and what I am doing. Many collies are seen running backwards watching their owners, but most are not really attentive to their owners they are expecting some action either from a toy or a ball. If the owner tries to get the dog to focus on something else the dog will not comply

unless it is to be given a more exciting toy than the expected one. If the dog is used to communication and conversation the owner will be in the dog's thoughts and not what the owner can provide!

You are doing this training in your garden or yard, where there will be few distractions, if any, and you are teaching more than just the recall. Your dog is learning its pack area, the recall, who is in control, and is focusing on you. You can keep allowing him the time to sniff or wander round the garden whilst in your area, this is his free time, but when you call him you have a right to expect his attention. Vary your 'game' by adding some lead walking, for this also brings the 'wait' into play as well as good manners. Before you test your dog's attentiveness away from home try some 'dummy' runs. Set up a situation that you know will attract your dog's attention, someone with a ball or maybe another dog, and now start your recall game again. You are explaining to your dog that you are to be the centre of his attention at all times. He can still have his free time and if you choose to let that free time include the ball or the other dog then he can play that game, but not without your permission.

When your dog understands these boundaries you are ready to take your training forward to the next stage. In the garden again and without the line you play the same training game. This time if your dog does not recall (and he should if you have given enough time and patience to the previous stage), go to him and bring him back to the spot you called him to. No praise whilst you are taking him back but praise when he is 'on the spot'. If the foundation training is thorough and has not been shortened for the sake of patience and convenience your dog will begin to be responsive. It can take longer to establish the recall with some dogs than with others, especially with rescues, but quite often it is due to cutting corners or not paying enough attention to the diet in order to sober the dog enough to make him more biddable.

Teaching the recall in the garden does not mean that your dog cannot go for a walk; it simply means that you do as much training as possible at home, for this is where your foundation is built. When you do go for a walk keep the line on him and do exactly as you would in the garden, teach him his boundaries and practise your recall. Your dog does not need to be galloping miles ahead of you; in fact, he shouldn't want to. When I hear 'my dog has a reasonable recall until he is a distance from me, then if a rabbit appears I just can't make him listen', I shudder. The rabbit is frightened witless and is probably carrying disease; the 'rabbit' may also be another dog or a sheep next time, and in the case of the latter either dog or sheep may not survive. I have walked for miles with my dogs, they are behind me when I ask and when we are on open moors they are invited into my space, where they enjoy themselves doing what dogs do when they are on new territory but they are never far away. If we walk where sheep are in evidence they are called back to my immediate circle, otherwise we wander on talking and thinking, quite happy with each other's company. If one of the younger members of the 'clan' feels it would like to try to design its own pack area it stays on a lead with me whilst the others have free time in my pack area. The youngster has quality time with me and also learns to earn its free time. If you were to go for a walk with a human companion you would walk together, one would not be two or three hundred yards in front; if they were they would not be very companionable! The golden rule should be – never ask your dog to do something thirty feet away if it won't do it at twenty feet. If you stick to this rule your dog will always be within reach. This is a rule I have always kept in mind when training and although my dogs are not educated for obedience in terms of sit and down stays and retrieves, they are biddable within my pack area on a walk. They will also recall from as great a distance as my voice or whistle can carry!

Do not be tempted to take the line off too soon; if you are in any doubt then the time is not right. A dog with a poor recall is part of a partnership that has a breakdown in communication so step up the quality time and make yourself important to your dog.

Free time. When dog and handler share empathy there is very rarely a great distance between them. They love to communicate and can only do that when they are close.

Praise

Praise is essential, but it can also undo a lot of good work if it is the kind of praise that has a similar effect on the dog as high-energy food. A job well done deserves recognition but praise overdone can cause demolition. Your dog recognizes word sounds; for example, the word 'leave' is a sound he may associate with letting go of something or not touching. The actual word will not have the same versatility to him as it does to us, for example to 'leave the room' or to 'leave until tomorrow', as he only associates the word sound with a particular kind of action. As your partnership progresses he will increase his vocabulary and the words or sounds he will be able to understand can be extensive, so the more quality time you spend together the better communication you will have. The

tone of your voice when you are teaching the sounds or the words will give an indication to your dog of what kind of response is expected. If you were to say the word 'no' in a happy voice each time you praised your dog he would associate our negative word as a friendly sound. 'No' to us is negative, therefore we automatically say it with a degree of firmness in our tone, which is the tone your dog picks up on and responds to. Once he has learnt it, if you were to say 'Bo' or 'Though' with exactly the same tone and length of sound, your dog would respond.

Further proof that a dog responds to the sound of a word can be seen in the example of a sheepdog who has have been trained with one dialect as a youngster then had go to a shepherd who has an entirely different dialect. If that shepherd is not prepared to 'language test' his dog he may find it doesn't understand a single thing he says, even though he is using the words the dog was trained to obey. If he is patient and tries a few different tones, shortens or lengthens words and alters the pitch of his voice the dog will eventually show some sign of recognition. It will only take a short time for a keen, well-trained dog to adapt to a sympathetic handler's 'new voice'.

This same use of voice tone has to be taken into consideration not only when training but also when praising your dog. If your praise is in a high-pitched or excited voice your dog will respond with an excited or 'hyper' attitude. At the end of a training session this is acceptable but during training you are breaking your dog's concentration and his 'work' mode, and a sensible educational game will change to a giddy non-educational game where he will try to take over command. Praise should be given in a tone that is proud, reassuring and kind. Pride plays an important part in the praise tone – if your dog is doing its best to please you then you must let him know by the tone of your voice that you are proud of him. A child who brings home an excellent report needs to know you are proud, and an adult who has accomplished a difficult task needs to know that the people who matter to him are proud. Let your dog know how you feel by your actions and if you feel proud, act proud. If you begin to wave your arms and talk in a high-pitched voice your dog will become excited, will jump up, may bark and may even give an excited nip at your lead or sleeve. He will be acting without thinking and in the excitement he will have forgotten how and why it started and he may even have disgraced himself a little. A Border Collie loves to please, but it is also a little 'work horse', so if you tell it

that it is pleasing you it will be anxious to continue working and pleasing. So keep your praise calm, talk to him and let him know what a good lad he is but let him get on with his learning. The time for fuss is at the end of the training session or the walk when he has been a good sensible dog. Collies are very quick to seize an advantage and if they get fuss instead of praise during, rather than after, you may find they have called an end to the 'sensible time' before you intended. Body language once again is the key to how to react to your dog and how it will react to your attitude. Look for that great give-away of secrets – the dog's tail.

Your dog's tail is a very strong indication of its mood and of how it is reacting to your voice and your body language. If your body is flexible and relaxed when you praise your dog your voice will take on a relaxed tone. If your tone is altered to a higher pitch with an excitable tone your body will become more tense and your movements more flamboyant; this will make your dog respond in a similar manner. If your dog is responding to quiet, relaxed praise its tail will wag gently, it will look at you and 'smile' its appreciation, its body will be relaxed with pleasure but its attitude will be one of continuation. If you encourage the flamboyant response your dog will not be satisfied with just wagging its tail, it will match your gestures by flying its tail high. This action will induce crisper body movements that in turn will encourage the 'voice' to whine or bark. Jumping or leaping up usually accompanies this and at this point continuity has gone. After spending a length of time studying Border Collies most handlers will notice the link between the tail and the brain –

when the tail flies high the brain drops low, and when the tail drops low the brain flies high! The 'dead' or straight down tail is the 'thinking' tail; the tail flying high is the 'gay' tail. If you switch off the brain by switching on the tail, your dog has not only changed its train of thought it has also registered 'free time' in its mind. It is unfair to switch off a dog's brain when it is being responsive only to switch it on again seconds later. It is also not necessary to create a 'switched on' tail to prove to your dog that you are pleased or to prove to yourself that your dog is happy. Tone of voice and pride are the keys to use for a happy dog and continuity in training, saving free time for something between the two of

you. No matter how much we love our dogs, they are still dogs; excitement in a pack of dogs leads to hysteria, but pride to a Border Collie is important.

One of the often unrecognized talents of the Border Collie is the ability to mimic; a long-term rescue of mine never eats his food without he gives me a huge thank-you grin. When he arrived years ago he was hostile, particularly when being fed, therefore when I entered his 'home' to feed him I always presented my 'friendly face' so he has connected the grin with the food and as a result has copied my expression of friendliness. A dog's grin is totally different to a dog's snarl, the lips may be raised but the eyes are laughing. Probably one of the hardest

Your dog's tail is an indication of its mood and this will often be a reflection of the handler's attitude. Quick, sharp movements and a brusque voice will incite similar movements from the dog plus a flashing of the tail in excitement, temper or confusion.

Jem is giving a reciprocal smile of greeting to Betty. Border Collies soon learn to mimic.

things to have to accept is that a dog will mimic what it wants to and not necessarily what its owner wants. If I had wanted to teach my rescue to grin he may not have been so receptive and if I had wanted to teach him I would have been impatient to see results, as this dog's habit of mimicking took years to materialize. Many dogs develop 'smiling' eyes – they are happy when 'their humans' talk to them and they return the smile they have seen so often by using similar face muscles to the human, resulting in a smiling expression.

Does Your Dog Really Behave in the House?

If you have any problem at all with your dog the answer, and the training, will be in the home. Many dogs appear to be well-behaved in the home until they are really put to the test and suddenly they are quite bad mannered.

Let's look at a fictitious case history with Collie and Mr and Mrs Negotiate. When Mr and Mrs Negotiate make a drink on a night Collie sometimes stays in the kitchen with Mr N. and sometimes follows Mrs N. into the room. When both the Negotiates are in the room so is Collie, having first pushed his way into the room (clever dog, he knew just where they were going!). If it is cold he lies by the fire, if it is warm he is by the door but most times he is behind the settee, so you see he is no trouble at all. Of course, he barks when people come to the door and he jumps up at them, he often has to be taken out of the room when visitors come, and he is a nightmare with other dogs. Collie is pleasing himself so of course he is no trouble, until he begins to take over the house.

A dog should bark when someone knocks on the door, but when you have acknowledged his bark and thanked him he should retire to his bed and allow you to deal with the matter. If the person entering your home wants to make a fuss of your dog make him wait for your permission before he leaves his bed. It only takes a few moments of your time, but in the young or problem dog it is worth it. When your dog understands the ground rules he will not take advantage. In the case of Collie, he firmly believes he owns the house – the dog barking at the door and trying to jump up at the newcomer sees no wrong in treating any visitor to his home as he pleases. These dogs have not been made to understand that they have a place of their own but they do not own your house; they can go anywhere in your house with your permission but they must respect your wishes. The remedy is simple, you spend time each evening explaining to your dog that the rules are to change and

A garden shed can soon be converted into an outside run for your dog, where it can play and dig to its heart's content without invading your garden space.

you learn to think 'manners'. If you are going from kitchen to room and your dog pushes past you, make him go back and wait, even if you want him to go with you, count to ten and then invite him to follow you. When you are in the room make him sit with you and be patient, move to another chair and if he follows make him stay, but if he stays make him follow. I call it 'tele' training (yes, it can even be done while relaxing and watching television) – it simply means that for twenty minutes you explain to your dog that he does not own the room and cannot do as he pleases. This is far more effective than locking a problem dog out of the way or ignoring his behaviour.

Should Your Dog Have an Outside Pen?

Yes. There is no doubt that a Border Collie will benefit from having his own private space outside. This does not mean that he has to live outside, but it does mean he has 'safe' freedom and his own privacy. Allowing your dog the run of the garden is no different to allowing him the run of the house – he will soon think he owns it and therefore has the right to deny access to anyone he doesn't like.

It may seem trivial, especially if your dog is basically well-behaved, but it is important. If your dog has his own area, which can be anything from a stylish designer dog run to a converted garden shed, he has somewhere to go where he can dig, feel safe and have some thinking time. He can still spend time in the rest of the garden, but it will be at your invitation and if you have friends or children round that are not particularly dog friendly, neither them nor your dog are harassed. As he matures he will probably hardly ever use the pen, but it is an excellent way of not only teaching boundaries but of giving your dog his own space and this is something he deserves.

If you have a dog with a problem don't look for complicated answers – the basis for all training is common sense and a Border Collie respects someone who makes it clear in the early stages where it stands. Border Collies do not respect weakness and they love you to negotiate; they are very quick to take advantage and they will soon take over ownership of your home while allowing you the privilege of paying the mortgage! But if you make your rules clear they will soon curb their humour to laughing with you rather than at you.

Treating the Problem Dog

If you have a problem dog you need to find out as much as possible about its background. It is no good trying to 'cut corners' – you will need to spend six weeks thinking 'dog' before you will see any real progress. You need not only to have a large amount of patience but have the confidence to follow your own pack instincts and apply common-sense training.

CHAPTER 9

Kids, Collies and Misunderstandings

Kids and Collies

Because of problems I have seen and the publicity claiming that Border Collies 'nip', I am tempted to say that kids and collies do not mix. But why should I be tempted to downgrade this intelligent breed of dog by condoning fashion? This sudden theory that collies see children as sheep and nip them is new; kids and collies always used to mix so what has gone wrong?

I grew up with collies and I was no different to most farm kids, we didn't have baby walkers so we leaned on the good old sheepdog. Before fast cars, dangerous roads and dubious strangers, farm kids were used to toddling around the fields amusing themselves, inventing games and making their own entertainment. A sheepdog, which would be not only their best friend but also their guardian, often accompanied them. These dogs worked for a living, using their instincts to round up sheep, but they never attempted to round up children, yet this intelligent breed of dog is now accused of rounding up children because it thinks they are sheep!

There is absolutely nothing wrong with the Border Collie as a breed as far as children are concerned and I am quite sure that many people are now going to disagree with me. The problem with kids and collies is adults.

A dog must be correct genetically and it is always important to check a dog's pedigree whenever possible. If there is the slightest chance that aggression has been put to aggression or a dominant line has been bred to a dominant line, then this dog may not be a wise choice regardless of whether children are in the equation. But the collie cannot be blamed for incorrect breeding and more and more breeders are using winning lines rather than good breed lines.

Most children on farms are used to animals and a dog is neither unusual nor a 'special feature' in their lives, rather it is part of their lives. Most sheepdogs that are brought up to work are part of a pack, they know all the boundaries and are well mannered. Most children outside of farming are not used to animals and a dog is often at the centre of the family. To say that a collie should not go to families with children is a very sweeping statement, but far too many collies have suffered from being placed in homes where they have been subjected either to maltreatment from the children or mental neglect from the adults. Human error again and not a fault of the breed.

Before fast cars, dangerous roads and dubious strangers farm kids were used to wandering the fields amusing themselves and their best friend and guardian was often the faithful sheepdog.

Kids and collies are not a new or rare mixture. Most of the old farm photograph albums have a dog taking its place alongside the kids.

Children brought up to respect animals can gain so much, and what better confidante than a dog, as it hears all and repeats nothing.

In general, parents with a new baby, first-time collie owners with children, a family with two or more children under the age of ten and families with a busy lifestyle should not be contemplating a Border Collie, unless they know exactly what they are doing. Taking any animal into your life is a responsibility and any dog is time-consuming, but a Border Collie needs not only mental and physical

The relationship for man's best friend must begin somewhere and it is essential that children are taught to respect a puppy and to handle it correctly, with gentleness and care.

A dog is entitled to its own space and privacy – far too many dogs are put in a position they will be punished for if they handle it nature's way. This dog is showing apprehension and is making it quite clear she is upset by the advances of the stranger.

The stranger does not listen to the dog and continues with the advance, forcing the dog to turn out of the fight and flight distance. The dog has now become the cat or the sheep, and if it were to take a choice, as the cat and sheep can, the consequences would be severe.

The dog, upset and unnerved, is being forced to make a retreat. The human being in this sequence is an adult but bending down to child's eye level. If this had been a child or the dog had not been willing to allow its pride to be taken from it the result would have been different. (For the purpose of these three pictures we have used an older dog who was willing to play the game to enable us to show you the effects on a dog. It is neither nice nor natural for a dog to be subjected to an invasion of privacy; Maureen and Gyp are now firm friends, but this sequence could not have been produced had Gyp not had sufficient trust in the author to do as she asked and had the author not been waiting to reassure her as she left the scene.)

exercise it needs understanding, and this requires time and patience. A collie cannot be put on hold for a day or two when baby and toddler are poorly, or shut away during the day waiting for the kids to go to bed. Neither can a collie be used to keep the kids happy, or for them to play with. If you have a young family and you take on a Border Collie you are taking on a responsibility, another being, and this one will not always be able to mix with the children, and for his sake not theirs!

Children brought up to respect animals can gain so much, in patience, kindness and an awareness of nature than cannot be learnt in the classroom or from books.

Puppies and young dogs respond well to sensible 'animal-educated' children and the association usually results in natural socialization. Unfortunately, many collies living with families are not able to benefit at all, for the children not only fail to come up to the standard of 'animal-educated', they see the dog as an extension of their 'possessions'. A child who does not respect his or her own dog will not respect a strange dog and this one may not have the patience of the family pet!

Again, the breed's temperament comes into disrepute through no fault of its own, for parents must take the responsibility for the education of both child and dog.

All children should be taught the correct way to approach a dog and all children should be made aware that dogs are not cuddly toys for their amusement. Even if parents have no intention of ever having a dog they should still educate their children in basic 'dog' awareness. No child should approach a strange dog and even if given permission by the owner caution should be observed. There is no such thing as 100 per cent safe and this applies to both dogs and children. The most well-behaved of children can show off and act out of character in company and the kindest of collies can take a sudden aversion to something that a human may not even have noticed. This applies not only to children but to adults also. A particular smell, look, item of clothing or a certain mannerism can either trigger an unpleasant memory for a dog or it may cause it concern. If the human being (child or adult) does not force their attention on the dog in question there is no reason for a confrontation. If the dog is put in a position where it has to suffer advances it does not welcome, it may feel it has to make its position a little clearer. Far too many dogs are not given respect when it comes to their own space and privacy. Human beings are selective, they choose their friends and have the right to ignore or avoid anyone who they find offensive or unappealing. A dog deserves the same right to be selective. A Border Collie is intelligent and proud and it also has a good memory, so it is possible it may remember something its owner has long forgotten. It may feel the need to be left alone. It may not feel the stranger who is about to handle it is a kindred spirit. Whatever the reason, if your dog 'tells' you it does not want this person's atten-

tion it is your duty to protect it from these unwanted advances. There are several reasons why you must respect your dog's private 'space':

1. This is the 'fight and flight' distance and if the dog has an aversion to someone they should not be permitted to enter it.

2. You have taken your dog into your pack and as such you are providing protection; if not, you are not a worthy leader.

3. You should always be aware of your dog's feelings and should respect them.

4. Your dog is part of your pack, so if you allow someone to 'molest' him without his consent you are betraying him.

If you walked down the street with a small child and a stranger offered sweets or tried to be familiar with this child you would be annoyed and protective. A Border Collie is handsome, lovable, affectionate but selective, and while strangers may fail to recognize the latter the owner must always offer the same protection they would automatically give to the child. Just as dogs vary in appearance so do their characters. Some are quite happy to accept adoration from a total stranger but others are more suspicious. So why should this more selective dog be subjected to unwanted attention just to please someone who is not even a member of their pack? These dogs are no different to their human equivalents. For example, I am not a 'huggy' person, I do not show affection easily and as such would find displays of affection from a total stranger overpowering. But I have a choice. If my dogs feel the same, I offer them the same choice I can take, the privacy of their own space!

One of the saddest cases I have dealt with concerned a lovely little collie bitch who wished for nothing more than to be able to adore her owner in undisturbed peace. Unfortunately for this little girl its owner had a marvellous relationship with a next-door neighbour, a person on whom the little bitch was not overly keen. The owner came to me very distressed after trying everything possible to persuade her dog to accept the neighbour, who wanted nothing more than to be friendly. Maybe if a confrontation had not been forced the little collie may have come to accept the neighbour (within reason) for the sake of her owner. But after being subjected to being forced to stand still whilst stroked, to sit in the neighbour's house, to accept the neighbour on her own territory and in her own private space, the collie finally curled her lip and offered to take a nice tasty nip if the advances were not curtailed. The result was a distraught owner who was now slightly afraid of her dog, a neighbour who no longer visited and a dog who no longer trusted her owner. This trust was destroyed in a very short time and it took months of patience to rebuild the relationship between dog and owner. This example can be used to explain so much – the collie who is attacked by another dog, upset by children or stroked by a person they find unacceptable will lose faith in its owner and in their ability to protect them. They will no longer rely on them and will take matters into their own paws, which can manifest itself in barking, nervous aggression, hiding, or total lack of trust and respect for their owner. The partnership no longer exists!

Ground Rules

Now that the collies 'pride and privacy' is understood it becomes a little clearer how to ensure that any children are brought up to respect this. Your dog will have its own 'private home' – this is essential – and your children (in the formative years) will not be allowed in to this 'home'. Some modern training techniques entail the dog not having 'private quarters' and the owner actually spending some time standing in the dog's bed. I believe this to be an invasion of the dog's privacy and a suggestion that children cannot be trusted. The theory is that should a child enter the dog's bed the dog will not enforce a confrontation. This also applies to the method of taking the dog's feed bowl or bone away from it at regular intervals, that the child should be safe if it tries to take the dog's possessions. However, there are two important points to be aware of:

1. If you are pack leader and your dog respects you it will also respect the rest of your pack if they are hierarchy to it.
2. Your child should be educated to understand your dog as a dog.

There will be certain areas in your home that your child will not be allowed access to. It maybe an office or office equipment, the bathroom, any cupboards containing valuables or chemicals, electricity, fires. Whatever the area the rules will be made clear, yet the same child may not understand that the dog's bed is a 'no admission' area. Why? Because the parents do not consider the dog's area to be as important as other areas, yet these other areas do not have a mind of their own. They may be valuable or dangerous, but they are not as vulnerable as a living being.

A puppy is cuddly and just the right size for a child to carry, but a puppy needs rest time and it needs to be able to differentiate between right and wrong. If the child carries the puppy round, why can't the puppy jump on the child's shoulders when it becomes a young dog? In a two-year period a child will still be a child but a puppy will be a strong dog and what was acceptable in puppyhood may be considered 'out of order' in the young dog. All dogs should relinquish their food or bones on request, but if a dog accepts who is leader and respects them this should not be an issue, and should not keep needing to be proved. If a dog has been educated to chew bones in its bed, or in its pen in the garden, and is fed in privacy (essential so it can eat in peace), there is nothing difficult in educating a child to respect the dog's feeding time and the dog's 'dining room'. A dog safe in the knowledge that its pack leader will sort out any problems will not harass a child who visits its 'dining room' uninvited. It will wait for the pack leader to resolve the situation and will not take matters into its own hands.

A puppy or adult dog must have a 'safe area'; an area where it can retire to if it feels threatened or unsure. This area can be in a particular part of the house, but if the dog has been used to a 'movable' pen in the form of a box or crate it can be given security anywhere. If there is a party involving many children, a barbecue, or at Christmas time this portable home can be moved to a peaceful, quiet area, maybe upstairs or in a utility room. If there is nowhere private, his cage half-protected with a blanket and with the door shut can make him feel secure, but make sure he will not be disturbed by well-meaning but prying hands.

A dog's attitude to children and to strangers is dependent on the education and the protection it receives from its owner. I have seen a well-behaved, sensible collie puppy try desperately hard not to bite a toddler who repeatedly bent down to the puppy, stared at it and then repeatedly screamed in its face. The parents, who had done an excellent job of training the puppy, saw no reason to reprimand their child as each screaming session was followed by a 'hug and tug, I love puppy' session. How this puppy, at only fourteen weeks old, had kept its sanity I'll never know! Had it only had a 'safe' area and had the child been as well educated as the puppy there need not have been a problem.

Why Do Dogs Round Up Children?

This is another of the 'Border Collies Do' myths. It is suggested that collies round up children because they are bred to round up sheep, and they will nip the children because they nip sheep. If my dogs cannot tell the difference between sheep and children I feel I may have a serious problem, and if they nip rather than 'work' the sheep I am not happy, for either my training or the dog's breeding is in question. Dogs do not mistake children for sheep, they see them as their litter-mates and as such they 'use' them to practise their skills, just as puppies and young dogs do instinctively when they are together.

To watch a pack of dogs 'training' youngsters and developing their instincts is fascinating. The class teacher, facing the pack, will begin a series of manoeuvres involving twisting, turning and dodging. Opposite him and trying to out-manoeuvre him will be the dog or dogs immediately below him in status and behind them the next rank down, so it will continue to the lowest in rank. The youngsters will watch and join in at the back of the queue, sometimes success-fully dodging and sometimes getting in the way of the senior members who will put them in their place with a controlling nip. There is no place in a hunting party for a dog who is neither nimble nor sure footed and the quick nip will make the youngster think before making a mistake next time it plays the game.

This hunting game has been explained simply but it outlines the puppy's natural instincts and its role in the pack. In your home it has left its litter-mates and its mother, but although it no longer has any dogs to rely on to teach it when a human acts in a way that seems familiar its instincts will be aroused. As these instincts are peculiar to it and not the human it will play the lead role. If the human is a child, that child is now playing 'lower-archy' to the dog! The puppy is searching for something to 'practise' its instincts on and if it has been allowed to believe that the child or children are litter-mates then it has found the perfect 'puppies' with which to practise. If the child plays in a manner that annoys or frustrates the puppy it will see no reason why it cannot nip, nor would it complain if the child nipped back. This is not peculiar to Border Coll-ies – all puppies will interact with each other in a similar manner. Whereas smaller dogs are often not classified into separate breeds but are 'typecast' as

'toy breeds' and the larger breeds are accepted as being 'dogs' rather than 'pets', the Border Collie slides uncom-fortably between the two. Not small enough to be a pet or toy dog and not large enough to be considered too big for a house pet, it is the right size for a com-panion without being too strong. There-fore if this breed acts in a manner that the adult human sees as being unaccept-able, a reason for its behaviour must be found. Its misguided working instinct may seem a perfectly valid reason at the time, but it is behaving no differently to any other playful youngster.

The Border Collie is quick and intelli-gent and can outmanoeuvre a human being with ease, and in many cases it has already been educated by the same humans to chase toys and balls and maybe even to tug something. In an effort to ensure that puppy and child get on well together and that neither is made to feel left out the puppy may have been encouraged to spend a lot of time with the child. The Border Collie does differ from other breeds in as much as it is a herding dog and therefore as well as the basic instincts of a pack dog it also has a strong desire to interact with a partner and to work. The earlier chapters explain how these instincts can be subdued or enhanced. The stalking, rounding up and 'holding' of sheep are all in the genes, but they do not necessarily have to be domi-nant characteristics and they all have to be controlled whether the dog is to work or not. The Border Collie is a sheepdog and to take one into a non-working home and not want it to show its natural instincts is asking the impossible. These instincts *are* the Border Collie, but they are not a problem and this breed is not a threat to children because of them. The problem is in the failure to make it clear to the puppy the pack position of the child and in encouraging rather than discouraging the very instinct that will take the blame the moment the dog displeases the adult. A puppy in a litter does not think 'these other puppies are sheep so I will round them up'; it sees them as something to interact with in order to practise the natural skills of the dog. A puppy in your house can either see children as senior members of your pack or as littermates to interact with.

Acknowledging the Dog

My children were brought up with Border Collies and not only were they sensible in their attitude to the dogs, they made quite sure when other children visited that they showed the dogs the same respect. At children's party time all dogs were in their own 'homes', be it kennel, dog run, utility or my bedroom. I never needed to do 'sentry' duty, for my children made sure the privacy of the dogs was not invaded. I also know that a little collie called Floss had a sympathetic ear for their secrets, sitting for hours listening to them and sympathizing with them (no doubt about having to live with me!). Not only was she their best friend and confidante, she was also a wonderful guardian.

There can be no halfway measures if children and dogs are to share the same roof. Either the children share in the responsibility of the dog's welfare and as such respect it, or the situation is open to problems, usually at the dog's expense for any misdemeanour will not see the children being rehomed.

Children love responsibility and are quite capable of sensible behaviour if they are taught from day one the importance of looking after the dog's well-being. All children, no matter what their age, must see the puppy for what it is. If parents talk to the puppy as they would to a baby the children may assume the role of 'older' brother or sister and will act accordingly. In some cases they may try to share toys or, if jealousy creeps in, they can become possessive and be hostile to the puppy or they may just want to carry 'baby' around all day. If parents talk to the puppy in the same manner that they would talk to a sensible child the situation changes and the child sees the puppy as having a mind and being capable of its own decisions; it is no longer viewed as a plaything. A puppy or a dog in the home is not another baby or a child, it is a dog and as such deserves to be given due respect by the children and not just by the adults.

Babies and Toddlers

No baby or toddler should be left unattended with a puppy or an adult dog, and as far as I am concerned this is not negotiable. It is unfair to subject an animal to the temptation of sweet-smelling fingers and mouths, which are at 'licking' level, and to the as yet uneducated advances of a small child who may deem it great fun having a 'live' teddy bear to cling to. I have dealt with far too many rescues that have been on the receiving end of such treatment to be even flexible with the 'keep them apart or keep them observed' rule. Let's look at a possible scenario – a toddler playing on the floor and eating, or appearing to be eating, can arouse the interest of a puppy that may just try to intercept the 'food'. No harm is intended but when the toddler refuses

A dog with its own safe area can watch children playing and need not automatically expect to be included. Children should be educated to leave the dog alone and to respect its home and privacy.

to surrender its possession the puppy tries to snatch at the hand; this upsets the toddler who screams and the situation changes. The puppy is as frightened as the toddler, but feels the need to defend itself and instinct makes it nip at the offending noise.

Screaming can cause a puppy or an adult dog to act out of character. All dogs have sensitive hearing but Border Collies are very susceptible to high-pitched noises, especially prick-eared collies. All new babies cry and the constant noise, especially when it reaches screaming pitch, can cause mistrust and suspicion.

A baby screams and the dog slinks unnoticed behind a chair, he is out of the way and therefore the parents need not be concerned, but he may be harbouring a grudge against the 'thing' that is making the offensive noise and making the pack leader reject him. If he has his own home and the pack leader sees his discomfort it only takes a second to give him his own security. He can have his own quiet time while waiting patiently for his 'quality time' with pack leader, after the baby has settled down. This way there will be no jealousy and when the baby becomes a toddler the dog will be used to waiting for his turn rather than feeling resentment. When the child becomes old enough to take some responsibility it will already be hierarchy to the dog.

The importance of the dog having its own private quarters is not to be undervalued, and when children are involved it may be the one place the dog can go and know it will not be disturbed. A nice spacious run in the garden is not only an ideal way for a dog to be protected from the humdrum of everyday life with a new baby, it need not have to even be aware of the noise. While the baby's needs are being attended to, the puppy or adult dog is enjoying peace and quiet in the fresh air, happily amusing itself until it is time for its walk.

Young Children

The first lessons in education begin at the toddler stage. If at any time the toddler makes an advance towards the dog or puppy the parents must be ready to intervene. A huge responsibility rests on parents, who have a responsibility to their child and its well-being, but they have also taken on the responsibility of a dog and therefore must provide it with the same security and rules as they will the child. Both children and dogs are very quick to understand the meaning of the word 'no', therefore it is not difficult to prevent a dog from pestering a child and vice versa. It should be made clear that toys are not communal, and the less toys the puppy or dog has the easier it is for it to understand it does not play with anything belonging to the child. If a dog has been used to an abundance of toys scattered on the floor it will see no harm in taking a child's toy. If a dog has a toy

resembling a child's toy it may not be able to differentiate between the two. The only difference may be the scent and the child's toy will smell sweet to a dog.

A child must be seen by the dog to be hierarchy and not a litter-mate, which can only happen if parents insist that the dog respects the child's wishes, but of course the child needs to be sensible. Children learn by copying and will often try to command the dog to sit or stay just as they have seen Mum or Dad do. However, at no time are they going to be unattended, so at no time can they issue a command without parental guidance. Once again a huge responsibility rests on the adults.

So how can you make sure your dog and your child understand each other? Your child must understand there is to be no:

- Pulling or nipping, sharing toys, sharing food, waking the dog up, entering its private quarters, staring in its face or screaming.

Your dog must understand there is to be no:

- Licking, taking toys, taking food, entering the dog-free zone (your child must have a space where dogs do not enter), pushing or jumping up.

Spend a few moments each day teaching your child how to respond to your dog, how to stroke it and how to talk to it. Teach your child the commands and when it tries them out on the dog make sure your dog does as it is told. One of the main reasons for a dog not seeing a child as hierarchy is the child's inability to command respect. Your child must be taught to command correctly and to take the matter seriously and your dog must give respect to this little human who is to be superior to it. However, it must also see this training in the same enjoyable way it sees all its training. Dogs are not children and therefore their concept of playing and of interacting is totally different to that of a child. A young dog or a puppy still has valuable lessons to learn and has to understand its position in the pack without the added confusion of whether the child is hierarchy or a litter-mate. All of your actions to your dog should be to reinforce your child's position as being superior to him, but you must also impress upon your child the responsibility of this position and the need for it to be a protector to the dog. As child and dog mature and become trusted members of the pack they will always 'look out' for one another and just as the child will offer the young dog protection so will the dog, as it matures, protect the child.

Misunderstandings

Power of 'the Eye'

One of the greatest misunderstandings regarding the Border Collie is the 'collie eye'. There is often far too much importance placed on how the eye can hinder the dog's performance, but not enough put on what the power of the eye really is and of how the eye reflects the dog's character and feelings. There is a saying that comes to my mind and is so very true:

> A man who looks into a collie's eye to receive an icy stare is but a fool.
> Be at one with man's best friend and through his eyes you will see his very soul.

A collie's eyes are the reflection of his inner feelings, they are the defence

Sheepdogs will spend hours watching sheep through a fence, which can encourage too much eye in some dogs and the same result can occur from too much toy orientation.

against predators and they are the power that can move the most stubborn sheep. A collie without eye power is like a musician without a piano; he may look the part but he cannot perform.

So what is 'collie eye'? This term is often used loosely to describe the Border Collie's hypnotic stare, which if not interpreted correctly can cause misunderstandings and sometimes maltreatment. A sheepdog can use the 'eye power' to turn a stubborn sheep, and it can also use this same power to 'hypnotize' the sheep, keeping it still long enough for the shepherd to catch it. Followers of sheepdog trials will have seen the 'single' and watched the dog 'hold' the one sheep away from the rest with the power of its eye. A sheepdog described as having 'too much eye' usually focuses on one particular sheep, even if it is working a flock, and becomes oblivious to any commands the shepherd may be whistling. This can be genetic, in which case it may not be easy to overcome, or it may (and this is usually the case) have been encouraged when the dog was younger without its owner realizing. Many young sheepdogs will spend time sitting at the edge of a field with their noses through the fence watching the sheep. If they were to gain access to the field some would chase or herd the sheep, only happy when instigating movement or 'work'. Others would only run when the sheep ran and each time the sheep stopped the dog would stop and almost go into a trance until the sheep moved again. In this instance the sheep is instigating the movement. If a young dog is inclined to show 'too much eye' it should be removed from situations that tempt it until such time that it can be educated to 'flow free' round the sheep, only using its power when needed.

A litter of Border Collies will all behave differently. When they are playing they will simulate the hunting game and most, if not all, will flow freely. However, one of the litter may prefer to lie and watch or stalk the others using its eye to observe, eventually becoming almost mesmerized by the game. It is very rare that more than one puppy in a litter will show this tendency as they are all practising for different roles and if they are observed carefully the foremost genes will reveal themselves. There will be extrovert, introvert, and a stalker, one who prefers to use the eye when playing and one who prefers to be more physical. This does not mean that the puppies are not of even breeding or are unusual, it simply means that they are all using their natural instincts to play the puppy game and each is developing its most natural skill. When you are buying a puppy the breeder should be able to tell you the characteristics which are coming to the fore in each of the puppies in the litter and guide you, not regarding which puppy to choose, but on how to handle the different attitudes. Past experience has taught me that if I see a puppy using too much eye when playing I should remove it from the main game and play a separate game with it on its own, encouraging it to move rather than trying to hypnotize. In all training you enhance the instincts you want to keep and control the ones that you prefer to take second place.

If a puppy is encouraged to play with a toy or a ball it will often become hypnotized by the movement of the object. This is the time to finish the game (or rather it should not have been allowed to continue so long) and to encourage the puppy to change its eye contact; if not, the puppy will disregard the human in favour of the toy.

The eye of the Border Collie should never be blamed as a problem or fault if a dog fails to come up to expectations, for human misunderstanding will have intervened at some stage to encourage the instinct which is being criticized. Border Collies not only vary greatly in colour but also in their eyes, and understanding the different eyes is a guide to how to be introduced to a dog.

'Fight and Flight' Distance

Fight and flight distance is the space between the hunter and the prey where the power of the eye comes into focus. Not all Border Collies have the same fight and flight distance, and it is dependent on power of the eye rather than size. If a dog walks steadily on towards sheep the point at which they begin to move is

the fight and flight distance from that dog. I can take a dog into the field and it will move the sheep when it is within thirty lengths of them, yet another dog may be able to close up to ten lengths or less. They have neither more nor less power than each other, they just have a different fight and flight distance.

If the dog's power is imminent at ten lengths the sheep will feel threatened if the dog is on the edge of that distance and the sheep feel they cannot move out of it. The sheep will turn to face the dog and a deadlock situation has arisen, for if the dog continues to move forwards the sheep will either turn and bolt, or (if the dog is still on the perimeter) will challenge the dog. The dog at this stage will be 'holding' the sheep with its power and will wait for the sheep to show a weakness. In the wild, the dog could now make its move but they are bred and trained to be controlled and the dog should allow

Moss shows his power of eye and his confidence as he faces a stubborn ewe.

the sheep to turn to move away. At this point the dog will not move to follow but instead will allow the correct distance to be reinstated before continuing to drive the sheep forwards within the area of control. Should the sheep choose not to turn and move but to present a challenge to the dog the tables would appear to be turned, for now the dog must either give in or stand its ground. A dog with both power and confidence will continue to advance towards the sheep, slowly so as to allow it a second chance to move away, but if the sheep does not move the dog will take up the challenge and if necessary use physical strength. This is the breeding of the Border Collie and it is this strength and wisdom coupled with the power of the eye that makes the dog so remarkable.

Just as the fight and flight distance is important to the sheep for its safety, it is equally important to the Border Collie, so if anything moves within the fight and flight distance of its eye power it may feel threatened. The vulnerability of a dog's eyes is not solely dependent on either training or confidence, although they do play an important role; the actual eye and its outward appearance reflect the dog's inner attitude and its response to eye contact. Knowledge of the eye and the way it can communicate is essential not only to help you to understand your own dog but to provide you with guidelines for other Border Collies you come into contact with.

Different Eyes – Different Language

Acceptance of the Border Collie's instincts is paramount for the breed to be able to retain all of its special qualities: to try to breed out or to weaken the 'eye' and the 'power' is damaging to the future

As the ewe turns Moss is ready to move but allows the ewe to walk into its own space.

of the breed. If someone is looking for a dog without these special qualities they are not, or should not be, looking for a Border Collie. It is not hard to learn how to understand them and it need not pose a problem even in a sport. If a dog is not interested in meeting other people and dogs, it may even mean it will concentrate more and perform better!

Not all eyes are the same. They come in different shades, they can even be different colours and they have different expressions. The one thing they should all have in common is pride, as all collies like to show off and even the shy introverts will have something they would like to tell the world about, but only if they have been helped to grow in confidence. The colour and density of the eye will give a clue to the depth of the dog's 'private space' and eyes are usually true to type.

A Border Collie with very deep brown eyes is usually a dog with a very soft nature, often a dropped-eared, thick-textured coat type; the pupils will be quite large and the overall effect will be of a rich brown. This dog will usually have very little power for sheep and will be inclined to turn away in a confrontation. As far as the 'collie eye' is concerned this type of dog will not present a problem, but the Border Collie instincts will be in little evidence as the dog has usually been bred of 'weaker' lines. A brown eye with a slightly harder colouring, appearing to be dark in the centre with a slightly lighter edge, will be a dog capable of showing a strong eye but it rarely takes offence if someone steps into its own 'space'. A dog with a much lighter eye, almost amber, usually has a very keen eye and most will resent their 'space'

Glyn is a blue merle dog with two wall-eyes. His breeding is of some of the finest sheepdog lines, proving a well-bred collie is not necessarily the standard black and white. The eyes can be almost unreadable, but the dog's body language has plenty to say.

being threatened; they are often happier if they are left alone to be 'one man' or 'one family' dogs. A 'wall-eye' is a blue eye and can often be almost unreadable. They are not unusual, but as they often follow a certain type they are not as common as the varying brown eyes. Most 'wall-eyed' dogs are either short-coated or blue merles, and a true blue merle will have a pair of eyes so blue they are almost unnerving. As merles usually have a very vibrant temperament it is often hard to decide which deserves the reputation of being 'a little over the top', the colour of the eye or the colour of the dog! Slightly more common but not always popular is the 'odd eye', one brown and one blue. I have never seen a dog with a blue eye and a 'soft' brown eye, the blue being usually more compatible to the lighter or amber eye. They are usually keen dogs with a nice strong eye, but not always fond of sharing their space.

Controversy often surrounds 'wall-eyes' and once again it can lead to an unsavoury reputation. One of the questions I keep encountering is 'are wall-eyed dogs deaf?' If they are, I think most of my dogs should have blue eyes for they can certainly turn a deaf ear! I believe this concerns the colour of the dog rather than the colour of the eyes, for it is possible for a merle to suffer genetic defects including deafness. Again, this is to do with the breeding, as a merle puppy will have one merle parent and this puppy is no more at risk than any other puppy. The problems arise when merle is put to merle, but if the parents are seen there should be no risk of buying a defective puppy. The risk area is if a parent has a merle cast in its coat, for technically it is a merle and should not be mated to a similar type, but it is also

Tess has one wall-eye and one light brown eye.

possible for the merle cast to be barely visible as the dog matures. I cannot stress enough that breeders carry the responsibility of the future of the Border Collie and owners must share that responsibility by making sure they are not encouraging bad breeding through doing insufficient 'homework' when buying a puppy.

Respecting a Dog's Space

A Border Collie approaches its work 'head on', it has confrontations 'head on', so if you are going to approach a Border Collie 'head on' you are not only walking into its fight and flight distance you may be walking into a confrontation. Never have a confrontation unless you know you are going to win and that in so doing you are not going to ruin your dog. As the first often results in the second it is wiser to err on the side of caution.

Approach a collie from the side and offer a hand for it to decide whether it

The correct approach to a dog is from the side and allow the dog to choose if it wants to acknowledge you.

A dog can invite its owner into its eye space, but the exchange will be friendly and not hostile.

wishes to meet you. If it ignores you then I'm sorry but it is saying it does not want your company, and if it is not your dog then it should have a choice. If the owner of the dog is quite happy for the two of you to get together and his or her dog is always friendly, still don't take it for granted (even if the owner has) that it will respond to you. Dogs are governed by scent and if you happen to be of an unacceptable perfume to them they may just take offence. If a dog is staring at you, don't stare back; this is probably just what it wants you to do. It is sizing you up and asking whether you want a confrontation; if you stare back you are saying you do. If you wish to look at a dog but don't want to meet its eyes in confrontation do as you would with a baby, wink or blink as your gaze passes over it and smile. Eventually it will either accept you cautiously or it will stick to its first opinion. Either way, remember it is a dog and as such deserves the respect it should have from someone who is not in its pack.

Never try to outstare a Border Collie, not even your own. This is a popular method with some trainers, but I have seen so much heartbreak caused by it and it is so unnecessary. If someone feels they need to stare a dog out there must be a problem and it will be one of dominance. If someone successfully manages to break the stare of a Border Collie, the effect is the same as the dog turning away from the sheep, and it will have lost its confidence and faith in its own capabilities. This may have the effect of making the dog dependent on the handler but that kind of dependence is not fitting to a collie's character; it should work out of love and respect, not because it has been made submissive. The dog that is made submissive by being forced to give way to 'eye' was probably not a very strong dog and therefore the extreme measure of confrontation can only harm it mentally. The dog that will stand up to a confrontation is the one that will not back down to someone who challenges it and this dog may not only accept the challenge but may also become physical. The results of such a confrontation may not only end in tears, but in the destruction of a dog that was only living by its own natural code. If a handler is confident, they can force the issue and win a confrontation at the expense of the dog's pride, which in most cases will result in the dog losing confidence. If the handler is not confident they will lose the confrontation and lose confidence in their dog. Either way, the dog will not benefit from such methods. A pack leader only challenges if he is willing to risk his life and a human being should be clever enough to lead without ever being in that position! Any dog I meet for the first time and any rescue or dog that has shown signs of aggression is never put into a position where it can either issue, or think it is being issued with, a confrontation. When the time comes for the dog and I to begin a training regime together the dog trusts me and it no longer feels it must challenge me.

The power of the eye must be taken into consideration when children are in the vicinity of a Border Collie, as not all dogs are used to children and unfortunately not all children are educated on how, or better still never, to approach a strange dog. A child toddling with large, unblinking eyes towards a dog can be quite alarming when it nears the fight and flight distance, and as the child is at 'eye' height a dog may see it as a threat.

Not all dogs have regular contact with children and if the first occasion is a frightening one it can make the dog permanently nervous when children are around. Not all parents respect a dog's privacy and I have lost count of the times my dogs have been sat in the back of my van at a sheepdog trial and I have heard parents encouraging their children to 'go into that van and stroke that nice doggy'. The dogs are quite peaceful – it is usually me who feels aggressive for I can see how easily these children can approach a dog in the wrong manner and cause an accident!

Chastisement

Water squirters, newspapers, jerking the choke chain, smacking, growling, shouting, scruffing – the list is endless and the dogs will probably wonder what on earth their owners are doing, or they are so used to it there is no effect. If you have a dream puppy and you never put a foot wrong you will not need ever to reprimand your dog and you will be totally on your own! But chastisement is another form of confrontation and if you are not careful it can cause a larger problem than the one for which you are chastising the dog. There is no need to start punishing your dog if it displeases you; your first action must be to find out the reason for your dog's behaviour. The 'artificial' methods are not natural to a dog and some of the pack theories are based on the human idea of the pack and not the dog's instincts. Water is not always available and in any case some dogs appreciate it. The rolled-up newspaper can be quite painful and it is not an action a dog will recognize. The choke chain is not even worth a mention, and the rest will

either frighten or annoy your dog if done out of context. The word 'no' is invaluable and if it is taught from day one it will be the best preventative you can have. Border Collies are mischievous but they are not naughty, and if they are stepping out of line it will be because they have not understood the rules. You also have to take into consideration the dog's willingness to please, for this often gets them into trouble. My dogs are regularly doing things which appear naughty, but they think they are helping. For example, I can spend an hour rounding up a flock of sheep to move to another field, and the moment the sheep go through the gate the dog brings them all back! I could scream, but there is no point for the dog thinks it is saving the situation. I have yet to convince one of my old dogs that the postman does not come every morning to train a dog, so he dutifully brings a small flock of sheep down to the yard in the hope I will be pleased with him. So think very carefully before you even begin to say anything to your dog for he just may be doing what you have taught him to do.

Scruffing is pointless; it is supposed to emulate the pack leader's action to an insubordinate, but I have yet to see one dog pick another up, hold it in the air and shake it. Another misunderstanding is holding the dog up in the air with its feet off the ground in order to make the dog submissive. Border Collies are free spirits and should not be submissive, so if there is a problem you must go to the root of the problem. Dogs may fight in the air, but this is while they are struggling for supremacy. The dog that wins is the dog that finishes on top, so cut out the middle action and put your dog in the lie down to begin with and make it stay there. To scruff or lift a dog off the ground not only requires strength but you have to win, and once again the dog will probably be dominant, and anyone scruffing a dominant dog can end up the loser. Any kind of show of strength, be it physical or vocal, does not stay at the same level. The dog becomes accustomed to it and therefore ignores it so the next time it has to be stronger. Shouting and growling may be what another dog would do, but it would also be prepared to fight – are you? If you put your dog on the floor, with a firm 'no' for the misdemeanour, stand in front of it (not towering over it) and make it stay there, you will have put your dog into the pack position and you will not even have raised your voice. Now *that* is strength as far as the dog is concerned. Don't give it the pleasure of your attention; it must remain still until you feel like taking notice of it. You can hurt a dog's pride without taking that pride away from it. You can sort out a problem without bullying the dog, and you can have a well-trained dog without it being submissive.

There is nothing nicer than a happy Border Collie walking free with its owner and sharing not only a conversation but enjoying quality time, a relaxed human being and a free spirited collie together.

Collies, Children and Chastisement

Border Collies can and do mix with children successfully and to the advantage of both, but only in certain circumstances and when both adults and children are in a position to accept the additional responsibility. It is important that there is both a 'child-free' and a 'dog-free' area and that the dog understands its pack position.

All children should be taught the correct way to approach a dog, should not be encouraged to approach strange dogs, and should never have close eye contact with a dog.

The need for chastising a dog means there has been a breakdown in communication. As we take the dog into our homes for our benefit it is up to us to make the effort to make our communication clear.

CHAPTER 10

The Beginning

If ever you have the opportunity to spend some time with an elderly shepherd, a genuine shepherd whose whole life revolves around his dogs and his sheep, ask him to talk to you about his life and his dogs. You will probably be surprised at his wit, amazed at his sense of humour and envious of his simple but honest outlook on life. Is it any wonder that the breed of dog spending so much time in the company of these wonderful old characters has a zany sense of humour and refuses to take life seriously? If you are reading books and training with the hope of having a perfect dog you are going to be disappointed, not because your dog is not perfect but because a Border Collie is only perfect if it is mischievous. I was told years ago that if I only trained for 'half' a dog then I would be fortunate to have any results at all. You have to aim for 100 per cent, be happy to achieve a little less and be delighted if your dog is not so obedient it has forgotten how to laugh. A very obedient collie is not always a happy one but a biddable collie is a delight to work with.

If you have accomplished what you set out to do, to understand that cheeky individual who enjoys 'winding you up' don't sit back to enjoy the fruits of your labour. For this is only the beginning and if you have educated your collie to use its brain it will already be planning where you are going to start next. There are just a few loose ends to deal with and then it's time to take a step forwards with your best friend and face new challenges.

Wherever you go with a Border Collie you will receive well-meaning but conflicting advice – remember, this is your dog and it's up to you how you spend your life together. As long as you are both happy, understand each other and your dog is biddable it should be of no concern to anyone else. Just as you have preferences when it comes to choosing friends and acquaintances so will your dog have its own likes and dislikes. It is of no benefit to either of you for him to have to suffer the advances of another dog handler who insists 'all dogs like me'. Listen to what your dog's body language is telling you and have the confidence to respect his wishes against those of a human. After all, it is the dog who will be going home with you!

There is no alternative for good training and that includes any method of 'de-sheeping', a phrase which has become popular to describe discouraging a sheepdog from working sheep. A Border Collie is a sheepdog by breed, nature and instinct; to 'de-sheep' is going against nature and the dog's way of life. To have a Border Collie and then try to take away the very instinct that makes it special is pointless and the methods used to turn a sheepdog against its natural instincts are not very savoury. These methods usually

Meg and Jay are having fun playing together. Take note of their tail language and the way Meg, at the front, is running almost on her side with all her weight on one leaning leg.

involve the dog associating pain with its instinct. A long rope used to tighten on the dog's neck or stomach, an electric collar, being shut in a pen with a ram, or ewe and lambs, are just some of the ways used to destroy the dog's reason for living. It is a sheepdog, live with this thought and use it. Don't take away the instincts, use them and channel them into something that keeps the brain working and the dog happy. Above all, if your sheepdog is likely to chase sheep it is not fully trained so it's back to the 'drawing board', find out where the breakdown in communication is and start rebuilding.

Border Collies are sensitive and after spending my entire life with them no one is going to convince me otherwise. I have met arrogant dogs, hard dogs and dogs that have taken a delight in issuing challenges, but they have all been hiding a sensitive soul. It's rather like imagining a huge soft centre inside a complicated maze; sometimes you get straight to the spot and other times you just have to keep going back and taking another route. The spot is always there, you just have to realize it and be determined to reach it. They also have marvellous memories and will act according to their last recollections of a place or incident

A travelling crate is an ideal mobile home for a dog and will fit inside most cars. Hope will sit in his in the yard so it cannot leave without him!

even though you may have forgotten. I can remember running Meg at a trial where, halfway up the hillside, I gave her a whistle to run wider. Twelve months later at the same trial and arriving late I had to go straight onto the course, and without a whistle Meg cast out at exactly the same spot! In this instance her memory served me well, but a dog with a good memory is capable of remembering the things that frustrate you as well as the ones that please you, so make sure your dog does not catch you out.

Try to get your dog used to travelling in the car as soon as possible and keep it quiet, as a whining or barking dog is distracting and can be dangerous. Not all dogs like travelling but many travel better if they cannot see out, as the moving scenery can disorientate them and it can also excite them. The travelling crate or cage is ideal and with a blanket thrown over it the dog can settle down and rest. Remember this is a dog not a child. It does not need amusing with games and toys and your dog will be far more sensible at the end of the journey if it has not been winding itself up into semi-hysteria.

Clubs and Competitions

It is not mandatory either to join a training club or to enter competitions but it will help you to meet new people and listen to different ideas; it will also provide both you and your dog with new challenges. However you choose to spend your time with your dog it should be the perfect companion and join in whole-heartedly with all of your plans. Maybe you will opt for the quiet life and just enjoy each other's company on long walks, answerable to no one and able to please yourselves. Or maybe you will join a club and enter everything available, in which case there will be certain rules you will have to abide by, so before you join anything or decide what is for you and your dog, spend some time sounding out all your options.

Few classes are designed for basic training; many class trainers are keen competitors and as such tend to teach to the competition requirements rather than those of a family companion. It is not mandatory for your dog to retrieve, do scent and perform sit and down stays out of sight for a given length of time, nor is it sensible to move to stage two if stage one is not firmly established. So if you are joining a club for companionship and basic 'dog manners' training you do not need to go through all the stages required for competition. Whatever your reason for joining a club sit on the sidelines for a while and observe, and if you are not happy with any of the methods or you feel it is just not right for you and your dog then search for a club that does suit you. There are many good clubs to choose from

A dog should not jump out of a vehicle as soon as the door is open; most dogs will treat the car as a home and it becomes their security.

There is no need to 'hype' a dog up with a tuggy game in order to make it do your bidding. As seen in this picture the nicest of dogs has remarkable strength in both its teeth and its body. A lead in a child's hand could prove the downfall of an otherwise obedient dog!

Border Collies love to jump. Gemma, displaying her skill of turning whilst in the air, shows how the dog's body is twisted and the whole of her weight will be on one foot when she lands.

Tip jumps almost vertically and when working will jump over a gate with his legs running as he lands.

if you make the effort to find them. 'Tuggy' toys are evident in some clubs and the method of 'tugging' is then used to wind dogs up before going into a competition by inciting the dog to 'tug' the lead. It is not necessary to 'hype' a collie in such a manner in order for it to compete. Ask it to do something for you and it will, if it has to be wound up to work it will not be thinking clearly. Don't be made to feel you are being 'hard' for not using toys and titbits – your dog loves you, not your pocket full of food.

If you decide you would like to compete ask your dog what it thinks about it, for not all dogs like all, or any, of the sports. You may think you have a winner for the show ring but if your dog does not like being 'handled' by strangers then it is not a show dog. Competition obedience, agility, working trials and sheepdog trials are all options and, although the latter is not an option for some, those who have land and stock may also be training for sheepwork. Border Collies excel in

whatever they dedicate themselves to and as working trials and agility call for strenuous leg work allow your dog to develop fully before training him for jumping. As a breed they are excellent jumpers and they love it, but few people appreciate the amount of strain that is put on a dog's legs when it is running. When it jumps the entire weight of the dog will be on one foot on landing. This is not just the dog's weight; it has the shock of landing and the speed of the jump added to the strain.

Twisting and Turning

Border Collies are very agile and they never give in. As a sheepdog this makes them incomparable, but as a companion it can lead to physical damage. They will twist and turn in an effort to catch or intercept a ball, they will run, jump and throw themselves literally into any game man can devise and they will continue past the point of thinking clearly. They will do this because humans enjoy and request it believing the dog to be well exercised. However, humans will stop children from playing to hysteria pitch or from 'getting too wound up'. They know an over-excited child will take some settling down and will probably be fractious when they get home. Think dog, think Border Collie and make him think.

Getting Another Dog

Should you get another dog and if so when? The well-meaning idea of 'two's company' can be a recipe for disaster where Border Collies are concerned. The dogs will be fine, but the humans can sometimes be made to feel a little surplus to requirements. I never advise anyone to buy two puppies at the same time. I breed my own pups but I rarely keep two of the same age, yet I have the facilities to do so and the time to manage them separately.

With family commitments and limited 'dog space' it is often difficult for the 'companion' or 'pet' owner to devote the quality time to one pup without having to find it for two, and more than ever when two pups are living together quality time is vital. When pups have each other for company it is far too easy to leave them to enjoy themselves together and put the training and good manners on hold until later. When only one pup is in the family the effort will be made to spend quality time with it and learn to communicate with it. Puppies have a natural pack instinct just waiting to develop and if they are spending time together they will learn from each other, interacting and developing their own status. By the time the human 'would-be' pack leader tries to bring some organization into their lives it is often too late, as they have already demoted him to 'chief cook and bottle washer'! If you want to be a two-dog family leave a gap of at least six

Double trouble! Two puppies of the same age are not easy to train when they live together.

They can grow up independent of you.

And in the end may leave you behind!

months and preferably more, although this depends on how well you are getting on with dog number one and how good a relationship you have together. A dog has its human leader for companionship and if the relationship is a good one it will be more than content with this. However, company of its own kind can be stimulating and, like humans, they love to share a joke but they must be members of your pack and answerable to you not each other. Time spent apart, no matter how short, will help them to understand who is the leader, and don't forget the rule of admission for this also applies to play time. When your dogs have had 'thinking time' apart they do not just presume they can run and play together – they sit with you and have a chat first and then you will give them permission to enjoy

their free time. Two puppies growing up together may seem a good idea when they are little and cuddly, but as teenagers they can be double trouble and as adults they may try to lead the way.

The Retired Dog

They really are lovely. These dogs have been there, worn the T-shirt and understand you better than anybody, if only because they always take the time to listen. If my old dogs could talk they would make a fortune in 'blackmail bones'. Old dogs have a quality that makes them as endearing as puppies and they deserve just as much attention as they had when they were young and agile. They will let you know when they want to rest or drag

Quality time is not just for the younger dog. The author spends time with Gyp and Kim, two old ladies who have earned the right to some special attention.

you out to play just when you were thinking of putting your feet up and the best thing is that at their age they can get away with it! The older dog is never any trouble; if it is loved and cared for it will keep itself clean, be meticulous about hygiene and if its health begins to fail it will appreciate all you do for it and will never complain.

Quality time is not just for the younger dog, it belongs to any dog at any age and the older they are the more deserving they are. However, with years of experience behind them their sense of humour is often subtler so beware of the tables being turned on you!

The only hard part of sharing your life with a Border Collie is knowing you will one day be saying goodbye and although this is not easy it is inevitable. I feel we should look at some of the questions I have been faced with over the years and how they may be answered. One of the problems facing owners of older dogs is if and when they should get another dog. A Border Collie throws itself into all it does; it loves life and lives every moment of it and also gives love unconditionally. The last thing a secure and confident dog would want is for its life-long partner to relinquish the joys of living with a collie. You are not getting another dog 'instead of', you are getting one 'because of'. When you should extend your family is for each individual to decide, but often the love of a second dog not only gives pleasure and a memory of youth to the older dog, it can be a tower of strength to a grieving human. It is natural to be sad, but don't let it prevent you from enjoying your dog. It never really leaves you, it is always present in your memories and in your heart. So you will never be without a Border Collie and if you have one now at your feet any that have gone before will be alive in the present dog's actions and in your memories.

Individuality

Border Collies never become boring for they are not typecast, and understanding one does not mean you will understand the next one you meet, for they are all individuals and need understanding as such and not as a particular type. Each dog needs handling and training according to its character and genetic influence, so ten dogs all trained to the same standard may all have been handled differently in order to get the best results.

If I introduce you to some different characters it may help you to make sure your dog remains an individual. At the time of writing, Hope is two years old and hand-reared; he is arrogant and cheeky, but this hides a sensitive, rather apprehensive mind. He loves movement and when travelling in a car he will pace and become excited to the point of being disobedient. If he is made to lie down and be quiet he is calm and eventually he will go to sleep. He is in love with work but because he has been made to think rather than to keep constantly on the move he uses his brain to get the best from his work. Skye (four years old) is always busy but if there is nothing for her to do, for example in a car, she will go to sleep as if she were recharging her batteries in preparation for going again. Skye loves people but, apart from her own family of dogs, she does not really get on with her own kind. She has learned that constantly trying to 'shave' each dog she meets displeases me, but she has also learned that I will not allow other dogs to go near her and upset her. With that understanding, if a dog invades her space she will allow me to handle the situation. Gyp (twelve years old), Max, her brother, and Meg, her two-year-old daughter, would all be quite happy if they never saw anyone but me. They never go to other people and they don't appreciate their advances to them. Max and Gyp made it quite clear they did not like trialling, but they love working and Meg is taking after them. Max and Gyp both have light eyes but Meg, who is not quite as stand-offish, has slightly darker eyes. To sell a female puppy out of Gyp for competition would be foolish, but they are unbelievably kind and loyal and as such are perfect for anyone wanting a one to one relationship with a dog. Pip is seven years old and ignores other dogs; if there were an explosion at the side of him he would only take notice if he were not already occupied with something else. He is very loyal and very much a one to one dog, but happily works for other people if I ask him to. He has light eyes and does not like anyone staring at him. He is a well-mannered dog, but if someone enters his space he usually treats them to an indignant look and moves away. Hope and Skye love physical contact with people but Pip never craves affection, he will accept it when it is offered but he would often rather get on with his 'busy' life. Kim and Kimmy (thirteen and ten years old) both love people and attention, both have mid-brown eyes and both are out-going. Kimmy is full of energy so her diet has to be carefully observed, but Kim is far more laid back and as such needed an extra boost of energy if there was much work to be done when she was younger. Tip (eleven years old) with

brown eyes and prick ears has always been full of energy and at times head-strong. Tip never tires and never refuses attention, he loves adults and children and anything that appears it may want to stroke him, but his energy in his youth took a lot of controlling.

So many different characteristics and such different dogs, yet they all work to the same standard, they all travel well and they can be taken anywhere without fear of my being embarrassed by them. But they will not all compete to the same standard and this is something we humans have to accept. No matter what you want to do if your dog is not cut out for it then it is not right for either of you. But there will be something that both you and your dog can excel at, all you have to do is find the right avenue.

Enjoy everything about your dog for even when it displeases you, and this is inevitable, the dog is using its brain albeit for the wrong purpose. Find it in your heart to be amused at his antics whilst teaching him it is the first and last time for that particular misdemeanour. Work with him and try not to fight him; many handlers spend so much time arguing with their dog that they fail to see the dog is often making fun of them. It is a big mistake to expect your dog to displease you, but it is easy to do so when you receive advice such as collies pull on the lead and chase cars. Before you know it, you are preparing yourself for a battle before it commences. Think of your body language – if you are expecting trouble your body will show apprehension, your dog will sense the hostility and recipro-cate with a similar body language, which in turn will make his mind hostile.

If you were to compare handling a dog to driving a car you could say that neglecting the mechanics, abusing the gear change and getting into top gear too soon will eventually harm your vehicle. But if you look after the mechanics, change the gears with sensitivity and drop a gear when the going gets tough you will get miles of pleasure from your vehicle. Don't expect your dog to run in top gear too soon, take your time.

A Border Collie is an elite breed of dog and needs careful and considerate handling to ensure optimum performance. When your dog is well-behaved and you feel you can take him anywhere you probably will, for he will accompany you walking, cycling, rambling, sailing, camping, in a caravan, a hotel, a tent. Your lives together are only just beginning and every corner you turn will show you a new horizon. You are a custodian for one of the noblest breeds of dogs, so enjoy every minute of living with your Border Collie.

Problem-Solving Glossary

Chewing

The more toys and chewy articles a dog has the more likely it will be to chew. Make sure it does not have toys that are household replicas such as brushes or shoes.

Recall

The recall must be a happy command and should always provide a welcome to your dog. Always make sure when you recall that you are in a position to make sure your dog takes notice.

Lead Walking

If you allow your dog to walk in front of you whenever he wants he will always presume he can lead the way. You have to make him understand which is his 'space' and that he must respect your space in front of you.

Hyperactivity

Hyperactivity can be induced by play, lack of discipline and the dog's pack posi-tion, but it is usually exacerbated by incorrect diet.

Noise Sensitivity

Although some Border Collies are natu-rally sensitive to loud noises many are conditioned to be wary or even frightened of certain noises by human influence when they were puppies.

Chasing and Destruction

The instincts of a sheepdog are herding, and chasing is not to be encouraged; many games played with Border Collies encourage the incorrect development of the natural instincts.

Collie 'Eye'

Many of the misunderstandings regard-ing the 'eye' of the Border Collie come about through insufficient knowledge of the power of the sheepdog. The 'eye' is a quality and should not be regarded as a problem, although it must be controlled to the degree of power needed in each individual dog.

Index